SESSIONS WITH PSALMS

Smyth & Helwys Publishing, Inc.
6316 Peake Road
Macon, Georgia 31210-3960
1-800-747-3016
© 2015 by Eric Porterfield & Alicia Davis Porterfield

Library of Congress Cataloging-in-Publication Data

Porterfield, Eric, 1967-
Sessions with Psalms : prayers for all seasons / by Eric and Alicia Porterfield.
   pages cm
Includes bibliographical references.
ISBN 978-1-57312-768-4 (pbk. : alk. paper)
1. Bible. Psalms--Meditations. I. Title.
BS1430.54.P67 2015
223'.206--dc23
                              2014048426

Disclaimer of Liability: With respect to statements of opinion or fact available in this work of nonfiction, Smyth & Helwys Publishing Inc. nor any of its employees, makes any warranty, express or implied, or assumes any legal liability or responsibility for the accuracy or completeness of any information disclosed, or represents that its use would not infringe privately-owned rights.

Sessions *with*
••• Psalms

Prayers for
All *Seasons*

Eric Porterfield &
Alicia Davis Porterfield

Also by Eric Porterfield and Alicia Davis Porterfield

Proverbs: Living Wisely, Loving Well

by Alicia Davis Porterfield
A Divine Duet: Ministry and Motherhood (editor)

by Eric Porterfield
Sessions with Galatians
Sessions with Colossians and Philemon

Dedication

To all who find in the psalms the gift of deeper, more authentic prayer.

And to our children, who have patiently endured their parents' focus on this project and listened to many of our dinnertable conversations about the psalms. May any seeds planted come to fruition in their lives.

Acknowledgments

The work of two scholars permeates these sessions. We are grateful for the work of Nancy deClaissé-Walford, which guided us to see the psalms as a description of Israel's history, and the work of Walter Brueggemann, which continues to shape our understanding of Scripture in general and the psalms in particular.

We thank Winter Park Baptist Church, Wilmington, North Carolina, for the privilege of living and praying the psalms in our life together as a congregation.

We thank Keith Gammons at Smyth & Helwys for the privilege to write; Michael McCullar and the Johns Creek Baptist Church of Alpharetta, Georgia, for the vision of the Sessions series; and Leslie Andres for her editorial work.

Table of Contents

Introducing Psalms ix

Session 1 1
The Path of the Wicked and the Path of the Righteous
(Book I: Pss 1–2, 9–10, 13, 19)

Session 2 13
Lament, Trust, and Worship
(Book I: Pss 22–24)

Session 3 25
Praying the Full Range of Our Emotions
(Book I: Pss 25–26, 31, 35, 39)

Session 4 37
Thirsting, Praising, Grieving . . . and Angry
(Book II: Pss 42–44)

Session 5 47
The Heart of the Matter: Authentic Confession
(Book II: Ps 51)

Session 6 57
Still Praying Even While Everything Falls Apart
(Book III: Pss 73–74, 84, 88–89)

Session 7 69
Turning to God as King
(Book IV: Pss 90, 95, 103, 105–106)

Session 8 81
Returned, Remembering, and Rebuilding
(Book V: Pss 107–119)

Session 9 93
Moving With and Toward God
(Book V: Pss 120–122, 127, 130)

Session 10 105
Prayers for a Full Life
(Book V: Pss 135–150)

Bibliography 117

Introducing Psalms

I had a lot on my mind when I woke up. It was before dawn, and already I was anxious about several challenges I would face in the day ahead. Still, I was able to stick to a habit that had been forming in me for several weeks—that of reading one psalm before our children were awake and before the busyness of the day commenced. I would read slowly, listening for a word God might speak to me and actually praying certain words of the psalm.

On this morning the words leaped off the page as I read, "Let me hear of your steadfast love in the morning, for in you I put my trust. Teach me the way I should go, for to you I lift up my soul" (143:8). What I needed most was to hear of God's steadfast love and to put my trust in the Lord, to allow God to teach me as I lifted up my soul, all of myself, to God. So I prayed this prayer over and over that morning: "Let me hear of your steadfast love, for in you I put my trust. Teach me the way I should go, for to you I lift up my soul." I've been praying this prayer every morning ever since.

As I reflected on this experience, I realized that I had been praying the psalms for a long time. In my fifth-grade Sunday school class, Mr. Brady taught us Psalm 56:3: "When I am afraid, I put my trust in you." This prayer almost prays itself now, moving immediately from my heart to my mind whenever I am afraid.

I remembered the night I couldn't sleep because our baby couldn't sleep and I tossed and turned until early in the morning. The next day I stumbled onto Psalm 56:8, which says, "You have kept count of my tossings; put my tears in your bottle. Are they not in your record?" God had been with me, attentive to every toss and turn. And God is with every person who cries in pain, sorrow, and fear, in a sense collecting their tears.

A prayerful reading of the Psalms gives us language to pray, specific words that help us articulate our feelings to God and that help us pray for our neighbors near and far. Sometimes the words are actual prayers as in the examples above. At other times the psalm speaks a word about God that we voice as a prayer: "The LORD is my Shepherd; I shall not want" (23:1).

Not all psalms use language as comforting as the familiar words of Psalm 23. When things weren't going well, the Israelites did not hesitate to pray their anger and frustration: "How long, O LORD? Will you forget me forever? . . . Consider and answer me, O LORD my God!" (13:1, 3). Such language does not seem reverent, polite, or "nice." Yet it is authentic, and as we immerse ourselves in the psalms, we learn to pray with greater honesty and authenticity.

The psalms give us language to pray our praises and pleas, our fear and faith, our delight and despair, our hopes and even our hatred. The entire range of human experience is given voice, helping us bring our whole selves to God. In these ten sessions with the book of Psalms we explore what it looks like for the words of the psalms to become the words of our prayers.

Praying Israel's Story

We look to the psalms to shape our prayers, but the psalms are not simply a spiritual gold mine from which we retrieve prayer nuggets that help us live our lives well. The 150 psalms were intentionally arranged to tell Israel's story and to help Israel maintain its identity as the people of God in a time of prolonged crisis. In these sessions we will pay particular attention to how Israel reflects on its own history in the book of Psalms.

After the Babylonian Empire conquered Jerusalem in 587 BCE, there was no king in Israel and the temple was destroyed. The best and brightest of Israel's citizens were forced to live and serve in Babylon, enduring what later generations called "the exile." When the Persians conquered the Babylonians in 539 BCE, the Israelites were allowed to come home, and over several generations the journey back to Jerusalem took place. But their home was in ruins, they were still ruled by the Persians, and though they eventually rebuilt the temple, it was a shadow of its former glory.

Israel faced the challenge of maintaining its national identity under the Persians, then the Greeks, and, by the time of Jesus, the Romans. Israel had to figure out a way to embrace its identity as God's chosen people and remain faithful to God in a changed political context. One of those ways was to look for hope and strength in the songs, poems, and prayers that they called *psalms*.

Israel had been writing, singing, and praying psalms for centuries. In this time of crisis, a group of unknown editors began collecting and arranging Israel's psalms in the form that we have them today. When read in the order that they were arranged, the collection as a whole told the people of Israel how God had been present with them in the past, taught them how to pray for God's help in the present, and guided them toward faithful living. Scholars believe the collecting and ordering process took place in the first few centuries following Israel's return from exile and, once complete, helped Israel "to exist as an identifiable entity in a world it no longer controlled" (deClaissé-Walford, 56).

Though each psalm has its own history of composition (date written, author, original context), all of which is hard to determine for most psalms, the editors put each psalm in a particular order to help tell Israel's story. The psalms were arranged into five different books, with each book ending with a verse that says something like, "Blessed be the LORD, the God of Israel, from everlasting to everlasting. Amen and Amen" (41:13). Each book addresses a particular era of Israel's history.

Book I (Pss 1–41) is almost completely made up of psalms attributed to David. Through this first book we "enter the world of the 'golden age' of ancient Israel, when a king of God's choosing reigned in Jerusalem" (deClaissé-Walford, 59). Book II (Pss 42–72) continues the emphasis on David and the Davidic monarchy, adding psalms from the Korahites (temple workers and singers, 1 Chron 6:31-37; 9:19) and ending with a psalm from Solomon.

Book III (Pss 73–89) narrates the destruction of the temple and ends in Psalm 89 with a lament for the end of David's line. God had promised that a descendant of David would be on Israel's throne forever, but with no king in Israel, it appeared the promise had not been kept. Book IV (Pss 90–106) seems to mirror the Israelites' time in exile as they began to shift their attention away from a human king and onto God as their king. Book V (Pss 107–150) reflects the return from exile as it "rejoices in Israel's restoration to the land and in the reign of the Lord as king" (deClaissé-Walford, 56).

Which Psalms to Choose?

The word *psalm* simply means "hymn," and the word *psalter* means a "printed collection of hymns" (deClaissé-Walford, 2). The people of Israel had been writing psalms for hundreds of years when it came time to put 150 of the best into one collection. But which ones would best fit the purpose of shaping Israelite identity and strengthening Israelite faith in the time after the exile?

With no king, no freedom, and a diminished temple, along with enemies within and without, Israel had much to complain about and many reasons to plead with God for help. Psalms of lament, voiced both by individuals and the congregation, were a must if Israel was to have words to express its full range of emotions. One-third of the 150 psalms are lament psalms, often speaking in language that seems startling to us: "Why, O LORD, do you stand far off? Why do you hide yourself in times of trouble?" (10:1).

Psalms of praise from individuals and from the community are frequent (146:1, "Praise the LORD! Praise the LORD, O my soul!") as are psalms of thanksgiving (136:1, "O give thanks to the LORD, for he is good"). Royal psalms ask God's blessings on the king (Ps 20) or speak to special occasions like a king's wedding (Ps 45). Some psalms celebrate God's glory revealed in creation (8:1, "O LORD, our Sovereign, how majestic is your name in all the earth!"). Other psalms celebrate God's glory revealed in Scripture (119:97, "Oh, how I love your law! It is my meditation all day long"). Some do both at the same time (Ps 19).

On its own, each psalm gave Israel language to pray, sing, and complain. As a part of one book of Psalms' five books, each entry contributes to its book's larger story. In the process, those who prayed the psalms were shaped and formed into people who helped strengthen Israel's faith and identity while living under the thumb of one foreign empire after another. In the same way, followers of Jesus who pray these psalms today are shaped and formed into people who love God, love their neighbors, and help their churches work for and give witness to the kingdom of God.

David

David was not only Israel's greatest king; he was also Israel's most famous psalm writer. As a great leader, "a man after [God's] own heart" (1 Sam 13:14), and a person whose example Israel needed to follow, it is only natural that seventy-three psalms attributed to David made it into the collection.

The superscriptions, the words in small print in most Bible translations that appear above the first verse, often assign authorship of the psalm, saying, for example, "of David." However, the preposition usually translated as *of* can also be translated as *dedicated to, on behalf of,* or *belonging to* (Brueggemann and Bellinger, 2). The psalms attributed to David may or may not have been written by him, but they came to be associated with him and are meant to be read with David's story in mind.

The superscriptions most likely were not part of each original manuscript but were probably added by editors when the psalms were collected and arranged. The editorial purpose was to set the context for reading the psalm. Sometimes the superscription connects the psalm to a specific event or time in David's life (Ps 51, "A Psalm of David, when the prophet Nathan came to him, after he had gone in to Bathsheba"). At other times the simple phrase *of David* reminds us to read the psalm through the lens of David's life. Other individuals and groups are identified in various superscriptions, and instructions for the use of instruments to accompany the singing of the psalm are often given. Though they often make reference to Old Testament people and events that seem obscure to us, the superscriptions remind us that each psalm is a part of Israel's story.

A Suggested Reading Strategy

We pray our story and Israel's story as we read the psalms. Israel's language becomes our language as we pray the psalms. Our lives begin to look more like Jesus' life as we pray the same psalms Jesus prayed.

We hope these sessions encourage you to develop a regular pattern for reading and praying the psalms. For centuries, nuns and monks have prayed through the entire psalter every week. Others have prayed five psalms a day to make it through the psalter in a month. Perhaps a more attainable goal for most of us is to read and pray one psalm per day. For the moment, though, we suggest you start by reading the psalms that are covered in each session, reading the psalm first and then our comments. Read slowly and prayerfully, looking for connections with Israel's story and for language that connects with your story. You may find verses that help you express exactly how you feel at the moment, or you may find words to help you pray for friends in need or for our world of need and pain.

We use the New Revised Standard Version of the Bible in our comments. Eric has written this introduction, along with sessions one (with the section on Ps 13 from Alicia), three, six, seven, and nine. Alicia has written sessions two, four, five, eight, and ten. It is a privilege for us to join you as we study and pray these psalms together.

Session 1

The Path of the Wicked and the Path of the Righteous

Book I: Psalms 1–2, 9–10, 13, 19

Quick to laugh, smile, and tell a joke, and just as quick to speak a word of encouragement or do a kind deed, my cousin Donnie was a larger-than-life figure for me. When I was twelve years old and he was fifteen, he spent a week at our house. We went swimming, played basketball, and talked a lot about Jesus. I wanted to be just like Donnie. Soon after that summer visit, I publicly professed my faith in Jesus and was baptized.

Since then, I've watched him live out his passionate love for God and for people. I've watched him deal with physical ailments and deep grief. I've watched him serve his family and his neighbors, all flowing out of a deep faith and trust in God. We're both pastors now, and as I listen to his sermons online, he never fails to speak a wise word to me, just the word that God can use to work in my life. For me, my cousin Donnie is like a tree planted by streams of water, a source of stability, wisdom, and faith that God uses to bless my life.

Becoming Like Trees Planted by Streams of Water (Ps 1)

Psalm 1:3 imagines a tree planted by streams of water that always yields fruit in its season. Moreover, its leaves never wither because it always has a steady source of nourishment from the stream. In the same way, those who stay close to God's Law (and stay away from "the path that sinners tread," v. 2) will bear much fruit in the good works God produces in and through them.

Law in this context is not a specific term describing the Ten Commandments or the other Law sections in the Old Testament. It is used here as a more general term, referring to all the instruction found in Scripture. To meditate on God's Law is to read it slowly, reflecting on it and mentally "chewing" on it to savor its flavor and seek its meaning. Above all, meditation is a prayerful way of reading Scripture, listening for God to speak a word to us through its pages. Meditation enables us to read Scripture as more than a duty or a discipline; it makes God's Word come alive as something we delight in as we listen to the One who delights in us.

Those who delight in God's Law are like heavy, weighty, immovable trees: "The wicked are not so, but are like chaff that the wind drives away" (v. 4). The image is of the farmer lifting all the wheat up into the air. The heavier, healthier, useable wheat falls quickly to the ground. The lighter, inedible chaff gets blown away by the wind. The wicked have no weight, no staying power, no standing before God and therefore will not stand in the judgment to come nor in the congregation of the righteous in the present day (v. 5).

The image shifts from weight to movement as Psalm 1 ends with verse 6: "The LORD watches over the way of the righteous, but the way of the wicked will perish." God accompanies the righteous on their path, but the way of the wicked is lonely and isolated, separated from God and the community.

Righteousness in the Psalms is not about perfection or being without sin; it's about striving to live in right relationship with God and with others. It begins not with right behavior but in relationships that produce right behavior. The Lord watches over the way of the righteous not because theirs is a perfect or sinless way, but because they walk with an openness to God's presence.

With no temple and no human king and in the absence of political freedom, the Israelites knew that in order to survive as a nation, they needed lots of people to live in right relationship with God and neighbor. The psalms taught the people of Israel how to become like trees planted by streams of water, and they illuminated the path people should take. They do the same for us. Psalm 1 serves as an introduction to the entire psalter, getting us started down the right path.

The Lord Reigns! (Ps 2)

In the Psalms no one stands taller as a tree by streams of water than David, Israel's greatest king and most celebrated psalmist. Psalm 2 tilts the psalter toward David by focusing on the kings that followed in his royal line. There is no superscription to connect it to David, but the flow of the psalm suggests it was likely used as part of a liturgy of royal succession. When a descendant of David died as king, his successor could easily have been installed with words like these: "He said to me, 'You are my son; today I have begotten you'" (v. 7). This statement "is a formula of adoption of the king, who from that point on is viewed as God's son" (Miller, 801). The king does not literally become divine but instead is anointed as the human vessel through whom God rules Israel.

A time of royal transition, when a new king is learning the job, is the perfect time for enemies to cause trouble. At times during the Davidic monarchy, Israel did have some measure of regional power and did exert influence over its neighbors. These neighboring nations and their kings are the ones who conspire "against the LORD and his anointed" (v. 2), the ones who want to break free from Israel's influence, saying to themselves, "'Let us burst their bonds asunder, and cast their cords from us'" (v. 3).

The psalm voices God's response: "He who sits in the heavens laughs; the LORD has them in derision" (v. 4). In other words, the God of Israel exerts power over these kings and will visit them in wrath if they continue to flout God's sovereignty. God also promises to break other nations with a rod of iron and dash them into pieces like a potter's vessel, making them Israel's possession (vv. 8-9). As a new king was installed on the throne, these words reminded everyone that God was the real king.

But by the time the psalms were collected and put in their final form, it was Israel that was broken and smashed into pieces. They were the possession of foreign powers. Once used to welcome a new king, these verses were later placed at the beginning of the psalter to articulate Israel's longing for a new day of freedom from their enemies. As they worked through the psalms, Israel would move from a focus on a human king like David to an embrace of God as king. Psalm 2 gets this journey started, introducing Israel and us to the "theological heart of the psalter: the Lord reigns!" (McCann, 667).

Praying God's Judgment on the Wicked (Pss 9–10)

Somehow the wicked don't get the message that their way leads to perishing (1:6), and sometimes the enemies of Israel fail to hear God laughing at them from heaven (2:4). As soon as we read past the first two psalms of introduction, we see wicked enemies everywhere. Often the wicked seem to prosper, and the enemy has the upper hand. Sometimes the enemy threatens violence (3:6), does harm through lies and slander (5:6, 9), and is a debilitating illness (6:2).

Always in the psalms, a wicked enemy is just around the corner, and always the psalmists appeal to God for rescue and for God's judgment to come upon the enemy. Psalm 9 speaks of a rescue already accomplished (vv. 1-7) and of God's justice being established in the process: "For you have maintained my just cause" (v. 4). "Just cause" in this instance refers to the psalmist's efforts to live in right relationship with God and with others as opposed to the enemy's refusal to do so.

Verses 7-8 read, "But the LORD sits enthroned forever, he has established his throne for judgment. He judges the world with righteousness; he judges the peoples with equity." The image of the throne of judgment identifies God "as the one who has the power and the responsibility to set things right in the human world" (Mays, 73). When things are "right" in the world, Israel is free from the danger of its enemies, free to worship God, and free to fulfill its calling to be a blessing to the nations. When enemies threaten not only this freedom to worship and serve but also their very lives and well-being, Israel appeals to God to enact judgment on the enemy.

When things are "right" in our world, people live in right relationship with God and with each other. The hungry are fed, the homeless find shelter, the lonely find community, the sick find healing, the refugee returns home, those threatened by violence find peace, and those who are oppressed find liberty. Through faith in Jesus, we enter a right relationship with God as our sins are forgiven. Through Jesus we also enter right relationships with each other, which requires us to work for justice on behalf of those who suffer and to pray God's judgment on those who perpetuate the suffering.

Sometimes God actively, purposefully, and intentionally judges the enemy (v. 5). At other times God's judgment visits the wicked through the folly of their actions. "The nations have sunk in the pit that they made; in the net that they hid has their own foot been caught . . . the wicked are snared in the work of their hands" (vv. 15-16). We reap what we sow in other words, and through the normal course of life those who sow in wickedness will be brought down by their own evil deeds.

Psalm 9 celebrates God's judgment of the enemy; Psalm 10 gives an extended description of the way of the wicked, centered in two areas: the way the wicked flaunt themselves before God and the way the wicked oppress the poor. Verse 4 reads, "In the pride of their countenance the wicked say, 'God will not seek it out'; all their thoughts are, 'There is no God.'" They are not doctrinal atheists who deny the existence of God but practical atheists who believe God has no relevance for the way they live and does not hold them accountable for their actions. Believing they are accountable to no one, in "arrogance the wicked persecute the poor . . . they seize the poor and drag them off in their net" (vv. 2, 9).

Against the wicked, the psalmist asserts that God does see (v. 14), does hold the wicked accountable, and does act on behalf of their victims. Only God, for whatever reason, doesn't seem to be doing so at the moment, and a plea from the righteous is required: "Break the arm of the wicked and evildoers; seek out their wickedness until you find none . . . do justice for the orphan and the oppressed" (vv. 15, 18).

Psalm 10 gives us language for praying against the enemy, whoever or whatever the enemy may be, that is working against the purposes of God anywhere in the world. Wherever there is injustice, wherever people suffer because of mistreatment by their fellow human beings, we pray against the oppressors using the words of Psalm 10, and we pray for God to judge the oppressors and make things right using the words of Psalm 9.

The same rhythm also applies in our personal lives. Using the words of Psalm 10, we pray our thoughts toward the person, the task, the challenge, the illness that is giving us fits, making us miserable, and working against our well-being. Using the words of Psalm 9, we pray for God in judgment to make the situation right. But we pray both psalms through the lens of Jesus' call to love our enemies. We pray that the enemy will not have victory over us but also that God will bring about reconciliation between us and the enemy. We pray that God will judge the enemy, but we also open ourselves to God's judgment, recognizing that sometimes we are the enemy who is working against the purposes of God. Sometimes we are the wicked person who takes advantage of others. And perhaps far more than we aware, sometimes we live as practical atheists, believing in God but depending on our own efforts to control our lives and the lives of those around us.

Authentic Language and Covenant Relationship (Ps 13)

When I was a little girl, my mother helped my two sisters and me with our Sunday morning preparations. Every week we'd stand still and straight while she put the finishing touches on our hair and solved any wardrobe issues. I loved this ritual and how it made Sundays special.

After she'd deemed me ready for worship, Mama stood me up on the bathroom vanity so I could see a full-length view of myself. In my petticoats and tights, I felt like a princess. Then Mama would say, "Now, if you act half as pretty as you look, you'll be just right!"

Many of us grew up with some version of this "act pretty" teaching. We were told to "be sweet" and, of course, "If you can't say anything nice, don't say anything at all!" Speaking kindly and being respectful are essential biblical teachings, which is what my mother was trying to instill in me. But "sweet" and "nice" are not how we always feel (even on Sundays!).

God created us to feel a whole gamut of emotions, from sadness to elation, anxiety to contentment, anger to love. Some of these emotions aren't "nice." The subtle message some of us received growing up in church was that (a) we shouldn't ever feel not-nice emotions and/or (b) we need to hide them or are "bad" when we do feel them.

In vivid contrast, the psalmists are authentic with what they feel, with where they are, and with what they want. Honesty in our relationship with God is the best policy—and, really, the *only* policy in the Psalms. After all, if God truly knows a word before it is even on our tongue (139:4), then we aren't fooling God with our "nice" talk.

Underlying this authentic speech is Israel's covenant with God. The covenant with Abraham (Gen 15), later adopted by the people at Sinai (Exod 20:1-8), is simple on the surface: "I will take you as my people and I will be your God" (Exod 6:7a). But like the seeming simplicity of marriage vows, the reality of living out the covenant is much more complex than it sounds. Like marriage, the covenant with God means deep intimacy: God sees Israel at its best—praising God and loving one another generously—and at its worst—turning against God and one another, cheating our neighbor, and sacrificing to foreign gods. As we know from the history and prophets of the Old Testament, God stays faithful to the covenant even and especially when Israel does not. Having strayed from the covenant, Israel stumbles and cries out to God; God hears Israel's cries and reaches out in times of need, never abandoning them. The covenant rests ultimately on *God's faithfulness*. Even when Israel fails, God remains faithful and loving. Consequences may—indeed *must*—follow, yet God's love follows far more powerfully.

Trusting God's covenant love, the people pray passionately. Every lament, every word of praise, every desperate cry in the Psalms rests in the covenant. As believers, our experience of God's saving love through Jesus Christ invites us to this same level of intimacy, where we do not need to "pretty up" what God already knows about us. Any cleaned up "God-talk" we engage in is likely for our own benefit, to convince ourselves that we are "nice" and "appropriate" according to misguided norms.

But Jesus doesn't want us only for sunbeams. Jesus wants us as we are: broken and beautiful, faulty and finite, limited and lovely. We are a mess; God knows that better than we do. We might try fooling ourselves with "whitewashed tombs" speech (Matt 23:27), but we are not fooling God—and we don't need to.

Authentic language made possible through covenant relationship is powerfully on display in Psalm 13. Verse 1 sets off a series of angry demands: "How long, O LORD? Will you forget me forever?" No pleasantries to begin the conversation, no praise to set the right tone, but four swift, angry, bold demands, which actually escalate in verse 3: "Consider and answer me, O LORD my God!"

This is the language of covenant relationship. Attributed to David, Psalm 13 shows Israel's greatest king taking the covenant so seriously that he lays out before the Lord all his anger and demands, hiding nothing. The covenant has room for anger from both parties, and in Psalm 13 the human party plays the assertive role.

But anger does not have the last word. In the first four verses the anger explodes, but once the anger is voiced, a movement begins that arrives at trust in verse 5: "But I trusted in your steadfast love; my heart shall rejoice in your salvation." We don't know if the difficulty has been resolved; we don't know if God has already provided rescue or if God has promised to do so. All we have is this statement of trust, which then leads to praise: "I will sing to the LORD, because he has dealt bountifully with me" (v. 6). It's as if David needs to pray his anger before he names his trust. It would be dishonest to praise God if he feels like God has abandoned him. It's the honest praying of his feelings, the refusal to hide the raw emotions in his heart, the bold demands made of the Lord that set him free to trust and praise the Lord. And the same is true for us.

Attending to God in Creation and the Word (Ps 19)

Though the language of lament is everywhere as we journey through Book I of Psalms, the language of delight first voiced in Psalm 1 has not been forgotten. As we arrive at Psalm 19, we now receive further reflection on what it means to "delight . . . in the law of the LORD" (1:2) and become "like trees planted by streams of water" (1:3) in the process.

Delighting in God's Law includes delighting in God's creation. The first six verses of Psalm 19 are a creation hymn, acknowledging that all creation sings praise to God in a voice that cannot be heard by the human ear but that nonetheless "goes out through all the earth" (vv. 3-4). The sun receives special treatment in this hymn, focusing on its rising and setting and the fact that "nothing is hid from its heat" (v. 6). The strength, vitality, and completeness of the sun's reach enable it to fulfill its created function and give praise to its Creator.

In the same way, the law of the Lord is powerful and contains every necessary instruction for living in right relationship with God and with one's neighbors. As in Psalm 1:3, the law in this context refers to all of Scripture.

In its perfection, the law revives the soul (v. 7). Meditating on God's instructions day and night generates energy. When one is languishing, delighting in the law revives, awakens, and sets one free to embrace life with and for God. The Scriptures are so rich, so valuable, so life-giving that they are to be treasured: "More to be desired are they than gold . . . sweeter also than honey" (v. 10).

The law of the Lord is perfect, but those who read and meditate on the law are not. The Scriptures, read prayerfully with an openness to God's instruction, help us detect our errors, see our hidden faults, and bring them before God in confession (v. 12).

It has often been said that we read the Bible not just for information but for transformation. Delighting in God's Word is meant to form us into people whose lives bring delight to God. So the prayer that concludes Psalm 19 becomes the prayer of all who read Scripture and who seek to become like trees planted by streams of water: "Let the words of my mouth and the meditation of my heart be acceptable to you, O LORD, my rock and my redeemer" (v. 14).

Life Lessons

Psalm 1 contains two opposite images, one of movement and the other of stability. Wise people follow the right path and reject the path of the wicked. They are on the move, choosing the right way to go. But they are also immovable, stable, deeply rooted, like the tree by streams of water. They're never stationary in their stability as they follow wherever Jesus leads them. They have embraced a deeply rooted walk.

Jesus calls us to walk into a world of pain and suffering in order to pray against and confront the enemy and work for justice (Pss 9–10). When we are on our walk and it seems like God is far away, Jesus invites us to authentically pray our anger and frustration as a way of deepening our trust (Ps 13). Jesus, through his own immersion in the psalms, calls us to meditate on God's Word so that as we move about in our daily lives, the words of our mouths and the meditation of our hearts will be pleasing in God's sight (Ps 19).

Wherever the path of Jesus takes us, we're called to stay rooted in God's Word and in prayer. We seek a movement that never wanders from its roots, and we seek roots that never keep us in one place but always send us out to serve. The call of discipleship keeps us constantly moving on the right path but always firmly planted like a tree by streams of water.

1. Who has been for you "a tree planted by streams of water"? How can you serve in a similar manner for your family, your church, and your community?

___

2. What does it mean to you to say that "God reigns" over all the earth?

___

3. Name a place in your community and in the world where all is not "right." What would it look like for you to pray that God's judgment would come into these places and make things right? How might God use your prayer to make you an instrument through whom God makes things right?

___

4. Have you ever experienced a time when God seemed far away? Did you pray, "How long will you hide your face from me?" If not, why?

___

5. What is your emotional reaction when the psalmists make demands of God, such as, "Consider and answer me, O LORD my God!" (13:3)? Why?

6. Many people find their attentiveness to God enhanced when they gaze upon or experience God's creation up close and personal. Where in God's creation do you find yourself pausing and giving praise to God?

7. What patterns, structures, and disciplines have you put in place (or would you like to put in place) that help you "delight" in God's Word?

8. Explore the image of a deeply rooted walk. How is Christian discipleship characterized by both movement and stability?

Session 2

Lament, Trust, and Worship

Book I: Psalms 22–24

In first grade, our youngest son received a free meal voucher for Golden Corral, a restaurant he remembered as one long parade of forbidden foods. But we didn't take him there immediately, which didn't suit him at all. So one afternoon, he slipped off with his voucher in hand to walk two miles to Golden Corral, located on one of the busiest streets in our city.

We didn't miss him for about fifteen minutes. I thought he was with his brothers or dad; they thought he was with me. A seed of concern grew into worry and burst into panic when we couldn't find him anywhere in the house or yard.

As we spilled into the neighborhood to search, frantically praying, a church friend drove up, calling, "We've got him!" Our youngest sat smiling in the back seat. Our friend had picked him up when he was almost out of the neighborhood and brought him home.

Relief, fear, gratefulness, anger, and a dozen other feelings coursed through me. Thanking our friend and God profusely, we hugged our precious boy tight and tried not to shake some sense into him right then. It all ended well, thanks be to God, but I was exhausted from the emotional roller coaster.

Enter Psalms 22, 23, and 24, which run the gamut of human emotion. Looking at them together offers insight into each individual psalm—a lament, an individual hymn, and a community hymn—and into how the three connect. Many of us can identify with struggling during a difficult time and crying out to God as the speaker does in Psalm 22. At the same time, countless people throughout the years have connected with the profoundly reassuring words of Psalm 23. And those who have been committed to a faith community can attest to the joy of the communal hymn, as found in Psalm 24 when all the people's voices join together in praise of our God.

Components of Lament

Notably, Psalm 22 begins with words many Christians will recognize from Jesus' crucifixion: "My God, my God, why have you forsaken me?" (Matt 27:36; Mark 15:34). This lament song starts with sheer honesty—none of that "niceness" many of us were taught as the appropriate way to talk to God. Once again, straightforward, authentic speech is the norm. Instead of adversity turning the psalmists away from God, it turns them *directly to* God.

The lament psalms offer honest speech, uncensored anguish, anger, and even bargaining with God. Though each lament is unique, they generally follow a pattern honed and crafted by the people of God over centuries (deClaissé-Walford, 24). The pattern reflects the people's covenant-trust and covenant-honesty with God:

Invocation. The speaker cries out to God to hear this prayer, supported by the historic pattern where the people cry out and God responds, as during slavery in Egypt, the wilderness, the exile. Underlying the invocation is the tried and true belief that the One who hears *acts.*

Complaint. The speaker tells God what is wrong. By giving voice to the experience, the speaker moves the problem from an internal locus to the covenant relationship with God.

Petition. The speaker asks God to do something to right the wrongs, usually offering a solution: deliverance from enemies, healing from illness, a return to connection with God and friends. No one is asking for riches, fame, or a problem-free life.

Expression of Trust. The speaker names why he knows that God will act, just as God has acted before in Israel's history and the speaker's own life. Sometimes the speaker offers "motivation" designed to get God moving quickly, such as reminding God that scoffers will think they're correct if God does not act—and soon. Such motivations underscore the speaker's sense of urgency: she puts all her cards on the table in presenting her case. God can be trusted not to abuse her complete openness. She can be fully vulnerable with her Creator and Redeemer.

Expression of Praise and Adoration. The speaker celebrates God's goodness and sovereignty. No matter how powerful or painful the lament, the psalmist ends with praise to the only Redeemer who can bring an end to the lament. But like the cross and resurrection, the good news at the end does not mute or negate the pain of the lament. Though resurrection is coming, the cross is still horrific; though praise ends the psalm, the lament rings true. Honoring the pain of the present and looking toward the hope of healing are not mutually exclusive.

Sections may be repeated or rearranged, but most laments include all five components. Inherent in the pattern of lament is the understanding that only God can effect change in the speaker's life and world. Therefore, the complaint must be placed directly front and center in the relationship between the speaker and God—the only place where the healing, wholeness, and new life sought after can be found.

Lament Fit for the Cross (Ps 22)

The fourteenth lament psalm, Psalm 22 begins with words that Jesus quotes on the cross: "My God, my God, why have you forsaken me?" The invocation and complaint collapse into one desperate cry, an overwhelming sense of abandonment. The psalmist cries out, expecting God's immediate help, but help has not come. The psalmist interprets God's lack of ready response as abandonment.

In just two verses, the psalmist captures the isolation of deep pain and distress, when we search frantically for a way to set things right again and no one can help us do so. The psalmist fulfills the human part of the pattern, crying out when in distress, but God has yet to fulfill the divine part of the covenant, answering with help and deliverance. The psalmist pulls no punches verbally: "Why are you so far from helping me, from the words of my groaning?" Notably, the Hebrew translated as "groaning" may also mean "roaring," which connotes not just sorrow, but an *angry* sorrow, or a sorrow with force behind it.

In the movie *Winter People*, an unmarried Appalachian mother is coerced into giving up her young son to the child's grandfather. When the child's father dies, his family demands that the woman give them the child to raise. The woman acquiesces only when giving up her son means saving the life of another. After delivering her little boy to his father's family, she returns home, bereft, and *roars* a cry of complete and utter desolation. Like Rachel weeping for her children, the woman cannot be comforted (Jer 31:15).

Such is the psalmist's sorrow and sense of utter desolation. Crying out day and night, he can find no rest (v. 2). Not even sleep can serve as a respite from this type of despair. Many of us who have been too upset to rest during a crisis, though exhausted, know this feeling.

Yet with the very next breath the psalmist reminds himself of God's holiness and trustworthiness through the ages (vv. 3-5). The collective memory of Israel calls to mind the people's past trust in God, when they cried out and God heard and saved them. In the present struggle, a moment of assurance comes from remembering God's past faithfulness.

But the next verse returns to the present struggle, expanding the complaint: "I am a worm and not human; scorned by others, and despised by the people" (v. 6). In the psalmist's time of need, others turn away, mocking his prayers for rescue, implying that God is indeed ignoring or rejecting the psalmist. Their words suggest that God does not and has not ever delighted in the speaker.

Again, the psalmist turns to the past, when God brought the speaker into the world safely (vv. 9-10). God has nurtured and cared for him since birth, according to the covenant. Within this unfailing relationship, the psalmist pleads, "Do not be far from me, for trouble is near," surrounding like "strong bulls . . . a roaring lion" (vv. 11-13).

With dense near-death imagery, the speaker makes his case: "I am poured out like water . . . my heart is like wax . . . you lay me in the dust of death" (vv. 14-15). This may reflect an actual illness, or the stress of the struggle may be taking a physical toll (Miller, 818). Others sense this weakness and gather like "dogs" waiting for him to fall or die. Like the soldiers at the cross would later do, they cast lots to divide up his clothes, counting him as a dead man (vv. 16, 18; Matt 27:35). Too weak to counter his foes, he makes another urgent plea for God's help. Only God can deliver him from "the sword . . . the power of the dog!" (v. 20).

Suddenly, the speaker turns in v. 21b, praising God for rescue, either sudden deliverance or one remembered. Regardless, the response to God's salvation is *praise*. The speaker vows to praise God to "my brothers and sisters; in the midst of the congregation" (v. 22). The psalmist will witness to God's salvation, calling the whole congregation to join him, praising God for not abhorring "the affliction of the afflicted," but responding when the psalmist cried out (v. 24).

Then the psalmist calls the nations to praise God, saying, "All the ends of the earth shall remember and turn to the LORD" (v. 27). Even the dead "bow down" to the God who saves (v. 29). The faithful will witness to "future generations . . . and proclaim his deliverance to a people yet unborn" (vv. 30-31). Like pregnant mothers crooning to their unborn babies, future generations will learn this song of lament, deliverance, and praise.

The psalmist proclaims a reality where the whole world, past, present and future, hears and receives the good news of God's saving love. The saving love of God spreads from the psalmist out into the world and throughout time, becoming as "all-inclusive as the poet can possibly imagine" (Brueggemann and Bellinger, 118). What started in struggle ends in universal praise—not because of anything the speaker has done, but because God "has done it" (v. 31).

The Deepest Trust (Ps 23)

As I write, our community is grieving the loss of a sixth-grade boy who was hit in the head by a line drive at baseball practice and died just hours later. A freak accident, every parent's nightmare, this loss is completely and utterly without explanation. Parents, pastors, and children alike are struggling with the death of this kind, accepting boy, a chorus member and all-star baseball player, a younger brother and a beloved son. Words fail us.

Our ancestors in the faith knew this kind of loss and have handed down God-shaped language that speaks to us even in our shock and despair. The hymn of Psalm 23 has spoken comfort and assurance in the lives of God's people for millennia. The image of God as the shepherd who guides us through peace and struggle reminds us that we are never alone, even in the shadow of death. These words create a "song of trust" (Miller, 820), the kind that emerges from a seasoned and scarred heart that has known the sense of forsakenness and the joy of deliverance captured in Psalm 22. In this song of trust, we hear our deepest hopes and longings—and God's undergirding truth.

THE JOURNEY BEGINS

God as shepherd was a widespread scriptural image familiar to the people of Israel (Isa 40:11; Ezek 34). Yet the vocation of shepherd is not familiar to us in modern America. The absolute responsibility the shepherd has for the sheep may be lost on us. Even the shepherd's name, the shortened form of *sheepherder*, derives from the ones he guides, cares for, and leads.

The shepherd's entire focus centers on the sheep, which rely on the shepherd for food, water, safety, sleep, and medical attention. The sheep respond to the shepherd's voice and the nudge of his staff, but tend to wander and stumble into trouble. The shepherd knows the way to safety and nourishment, what the sheep long for most and what the shepherd longs to give them most.

The opening words reflect a deep awareness of God's intent, focused care (v. 1). The speaker claims his dependence, knowing God provides for his needs, just as the shepherd provides for the sheep. Echoed here is God's care for the Israelites in the wilderness, when manna, quail, and water from the rock sustained, and fire and cloud guided (Exod 13:17-22; 16; 17; Miller, 820).

The shepherd guides the speaker to "lie down in green pastures," a place of abundance and peace. There, the speaker may rest, knowing that sustenance and "still waters," where thirst can be quenched safely and easily, are at hand. In a place of nourishment and respite, God "restores" his soul (vv. 2-3).

The shepherd leads the speaker in "right paths" (v. 3), ways that follow God's commandments and lead to right relationships with God and others (Prov 3:5-6). Yet even while following God's paths, the psalmist encounters difficult terrain: "Even though I walk through the darkest valley, I will fear no evil; for you are with me; your rod and your staff—they comfort me" (v. 4). The psalmist captures the reality of living in a broken world where pain, suffering, and distress are unavoidable. Still, God is present, intimately so, as the speaker changes from talking about God to talking *to* God, from "he" to "you."

Modern-day shepherd Phillip Keller notes that it is in the dark valleys that the shepherd is closest to the sheep, close enough so his near presence and voice reassure the sheep. As winter drives the flock off the mountains and into the valley, the sheep are "in intimate contact with" the shepherd, "under his most personal attention day and night" (Keller, 98). In the valley, the shepherd is closer than ever to his flock.

Ever watchful, the shepherd uses the rod and staff to protect and guide his sheep. The rod is a defensive tool used to "fend off wild animals" that prey on the sheep (Miller, 820). The staff is the traditional shepherd's crook that guides the sheep, turning the wanderer's neck and head back to the right direction. Both tools help the shepherd guide the sheep through the valley and then onto higher ground.

In verse 5 the scene shifts to God as host of a large dinner. Like the shepherd, the host provides food, drink, and safety. Even enemies are defused at God's table, no longer threats, but quiet supplicants at God's banquet. They watch as God anoints the speaker's head with oil, a custom reserved for an honored guest (Miller, 820). The overflowing cup reflects God's generous goodness and faithfulness, a free gift offered in love (v. 5b).

God's goodness and mercy shall follow the psalmist for the rest of his life (v. 6). Instead of being pursued by enemies, the speaker is now pursued by God's goodness (Miller, 820). The speaker will enjoy spiritual well-being "all the days of my life," dwelling in the house of the Lord "my whole life long" (v. 6).

Underlying the psalm are the speaker's and community's covenant experience with God. Through good times and bad, God has provided nurture, rest, protection, and presence. God's care and reassurance in the "darkest valley" do not erase the struggle of the valley, but ensure that the valley is not the last word. The banquet table, abundant and welcoming, is God's last word for the speaker and the community of faith. These holy words of trust penned thousands of years ago still reassure us today, echoing our own experience of and deepest beliefs about the God who is true to the new covenant in Jesus Christ.

Worship! (Ps 24)

Following a psalm of lament and a hymn of thanksgiving, the psalter offers a community hymn of praise. Embedded in this trajectory is the awareness that our personal laments and thanksgiving belong in our life as a community of faith. We are not persons following God but the *people of God*, bound by God's loving faithfulness, our shared trials and triumphs, and our worship of God.

Psalm 24 was "sung during worship on holy days," likely during the "three great pilgrimage festivals of ancient Israel: the Feasts of Unleavened Bread and Passover, First Fruits (Pentecost), and Tabernacles (or booths)" (deClaissé-Walford, 20, 40). Later, after returning from the Babylonian exile, Israel's leaders combined Psalm 24 with other creation psalms in the *Tamid*, a collection read as a part of the daily service at the temple (deClaissé-Walford, 40).

This particular hymn lifts up the joy of coming together to worship as God's people. The mood is highly celebratory, similar in tone and spirit to an Easter hymn. The psalms consider praise an essential part of individual and communal health. Just as we cry out to God in pain, we also cry out to God in joy—lament *and* praise are authentic worship.

Psalm 24 forms a liturgy of call and response for entering the temple. A temple leader and the people trade off speaking lines of praise. Just as a modern hymn has a pattern of chorus and verses, ancient hymns were also patterned to emphasize certain points via repetition, while exploring the theme in other parts.

Psalm 24 begins with the creation claim that "the earth is the LORD's and all that is in it, the world, and those who live in it" (v. 1). The speaker asserts God's sovereignty using a poetic form called parallelism, found throughout the book of Psalms. Here, the psalmist uses "synonymous parallelism," where the first line makes a statement, "The earth is the LORD's and everything in it," and the second line echoes the theme using different words, "the world, and those who live in it" (McCann, 652). The repetition of ideas in different words emphasizes the point while adding layers of meaning.

Verse 2 explains why the earth is the Lord's: "for he has founded it on the seas, and established it on the rivers." Again, we hear the parallel: The Lord "founded/established" the earth on the "seas/rivers"; therefore, "the earth is the LORD's and everything in it." Together, verses 1-2 offer a confession about the Creator.

The psalmist shifts to a question about God's worshipers: "Who shall ascend the hill of the LORD?" The next line parallels the first, asking, "And who shall stand in his holy place?" (v. 3). The answer comes in parallel: "Those who have clean hands and pure hearts, who do not lift up their souls to what is false, and do not swear deceitfully" (v. 4). The people's part of the covenant is to be God's "priestly kingdom and a holy nation" (Exod 19:6), living according to the Law and the prophets.

Clearly, this does not mean that the people of God are blameless and without fault—as anyone with even a passing knowledge of the Bible or the church can attest. Rather, the people of God understand that God's forgiveness is readily available and accessible when we fail to love God and each other. Entering the temple together includes acknowledging our failures and faults, offering them to God, asking forgiveness, and accepting the gift of our cleansing (see Ps 51). The "clean hands and pure hearts" are constantly being cleansed and purified by God.

Forgiven and cleansed, the people gather to praise the one who pardons and delivers. Shaped by God and nurtured by one another, the people will "receive blessing from the LORD" (v. 5). They "seek the face of the God of Jacob" (v. 6), who is faithful from generation to generation.

Verse 7 shifts to an image of the Lord entering the city and temple, likely "by means of the ark of the covenant" (Miller, 820). The ark was the intricately crafted chest that housed the tablets of the Ten Commandments (Exod 25:10-16), understood to be the "divine throne or its footstool" (Greenstein, 125). The ark was Israel's most sacred religious object, housed in the temple's inner sanctuary, the Holy of Holies (1 Kgs 6:19).

The ark-bearers, or those representing them, call out, "Lift up your heads, O gates! and be lifted up, O ancient doors! that the King of glory may come in" (v. 7). The speakers personify the gates and doors of Jerusalem and the temple by demanding that they "wake up" (Peterson, *The Message*, 805) and prepare to receive God's presence. The presence of God demands that even the gates and doors respond, just as the people respond with confession and repentance, celebration and praise.

The doorkeepers ask, "Who is the King of glory?" allowing the people to answer, "The LORD, strong and mighty, the LORD, mighty in battle" (v. 8). This is their collective witness of all God has done for them throughout history. Amid loss and grief, God has been faithful. Their response is worship, joyful and praise-filled.

Echoed here is the scene of King David bringing the ark into Jerusalem (2 Sam 6:12-15; Miller, 821). With sheer abandon, David dances "before the LORD with all his might" (2 Sam 6:14), accompanied by trumpet sound and the people's shouting. Offering sacrifices to God, David blesses the people and distributes food to everyone. It is a scene of true celebration, abandon, and abundance.

In this spirit, the psalmist repeats the question/answer pattern to affirm the King of glory again. As one, they testify to God's goodness, faithfulness, and love, just as we do today as we gather for worship. In our hymns, responsive readings, Scripture readings, and prayers, we join as one, testifying to the King of glory.

Life Lessons

As God's children, we are given the gift of life to share it—with God and each other. We choose how deeply we engage in life and share it. But we do not choose *that* life happens to us, life happens whether we want it to or not. Tornadoes blow through town. Love blows through our hearts. The Spirit blows away an old hurt and brings healing in its place. Change blows in and rearranges our priorities just when we thought we had everything settled.

Psalms 22, 23, and 24 record achingly honest, desperately human responses to what life has brought the psalmists: despair, grief, praise, trust, remembrance, exhaustion, joy, hope, anguish. All of these feelings and experiences are folded into prayer, placed—even shoved—into the speakers' relationship with God. Real life, real feelings, unedited for public consumption, spill onto the pages, surprising us with their no-holds-barred approach.

These ancient songs are our stories. We know these feelings, though we may not express them so clearly or so poetically. Everyday life, with its comfortable routines and constant anxieties, often dulls us to life's extremes. But when we are in the valley, when we feel "poured out like water" (22:14), we reach for God's rod and staff to comfort us. When we come with the congregation to worship on a day of celebration, our hearts rise with joy to "receive blessing from the LORD" (24:5). Psalms like these provide us with language that matches the depth and breadth of human experience. All we need to do is claim them.

1. Consider the honest, heart-wrenching lament of Psalm 22. Where is there room in our world for this kind of truth-telling about our grief, loss, and anguish?

_____
_____
_____
_____
_____

2. Think back to a time of deep loss in your life. How did your experience of loss affect your prayer life and your relationships?

_____
_____
_____
_____
_____

3. How did you feel when God brought that deep mourning to an end? How would you describe that to someone else or offer your thanksgiving in praise to God?

_____
_____
_____
_____
_____

4. When has Psalm 23 brought comfort or hope in your life experience? When have you experienced this kind of deep trust and hope in God?

_____
_____
_____
_____
_____

Lament, Trust, and Worship

5. Which images from Psalm 23 speak most clearly to you? How might you incorporate images or verses from this psalm into your daily prayer life?

6. When have you experienced the deep joy of corporate worship expressed in Psalm 24? What was that like?

7. How integral is corporate worship in your life? What aspects of worship help you best praise God as "the King of glory"?

Session 3

Praying the Full Range of Our Emotions

Book I: Psalms 25–26, 31, 35, 39

For this session we remain in Book I, which is dominated by psalms described in their superscriptions as "of David." In associating these psalms with the voice of David, Israel finds its own voice. David's heart is an open book for Israel, with every emotion expressed, little restraint practiced, and not much of a sieve between heart and mouth. When David thinks it and feels it, he says it and prays it. The psalms give us language to do the same.

Psalm 25 gives us language to voice our willingness to learn and to wait. Psalm 26 gives us language to speak up for ourselves when we have been treated unfairly, putting aside a false humility and boldly making our case before God that we are in the right. Psalm 31 gives us permission to whine and feel sorry for ourselves on occasion. Psalm 35 shows us that even our hate must be prayed. And Psalm 39 gives us permission to ask God to turn away from us when it feels like God's judgment is too much to bear.

Teach Me! (Ps 25)

As winter turned to spring and the grass started to grow, I reluctantly entered the grass-cutting season. I'm not a good maintenance person, but I did change the oil as the season began. Still, the engine became quieter and quieter with each cut, and it wasn't a good quiet—the quieter the engine, the slower the movement of the blade. It wasn't long before I was moving at a snail's pace; it was the only way the blade had a chance of cutting even the thinnest blade of grass.

I pulled out the instruction manual and started looking for help. Air filter? I hadn't looked at the air filter. When I did, the amount of dust that fell at my feet was astounding, and I spent a good ten minutes cleaning it. With a clean air filter, the engine cranked louder than ever, strong and robust, able to cut the toughest weed all because of a free flow of air.

So often something obstructs the "air flow" in our relationship with God. Sin, the ways in which we fall short in loving God and in loving our neighbors, is a huge flow blocker, so we pray, "For your name's sake, O LORD, pardon my guilt, for it is great" (v. 11).

The desire to be in control is another primary flow blocker for many of us. We think we know what to do and how to do it. We may ask God to give us strength, but we're still running the show. We may even find some success, yet all the while the air of God's Spirit is being blocked by our unwillingness to place our lives fully in God's hands.

But we can pray some openness into our lives and pray ourselves into having a teachable spirit: "Make me to know your ways, O LORD; teach me your paths. Lead me in your truth, and teach me, for you are the God of my salvation" (vv. 4-5). It's not that we reject the important work of planning and preparation as we enter our days at home, at work, at school, or at church. Instead, to pray in the morning "Make me to know your ways" and then to repeat the prayer throughout the day allows God to shape our plans and keeps our spirits open to God's guidance as the day unfolds. Seeking to control our days eventually exhausts us because it can't be done; living the day while praying "teach me your paths" actually gives us far more energy as we participate in what God is doing in and through us.

The more teachable we become the less anxious and the more patient we become. We can pray the end of verse 5 truthfully: "for you I wait all day long." Waiting is not passive; rather, it is an active anticipation of what God is about to do. It may take a long time before the anticipated divine action occurs, but we are learning from God as we wait and walking the paths that the Lord is teaching us.

Waiting is a crucial component of learning. Too often we want to learn quickly, consuming God's lessons like a fast-food meal so we can get to the next lesson as fast as possible. But "teach me your paths" is not a prayer we pray once and then we're done, with God imparting to our souls all the lessons we need from then on in one instantaneous transaction. We pray these prayers daily over a lifetime, learning each day's lessons on that day and waiting until tomorrow and the next day and the next month and the next year to learn future insights about the ways, paths, and truth of the Lord.

Vindicate Me! (Ps 26)

Psalm 25 is the voice of humility, with the psalmist giving up control and waiting for the Lord to teach and lead. Psalm 26 is the voice of assertiveness—that of someone making a case of personally being in the right. It's not a moment to be taught, but a moment for personal defense before God.

The danger is unclear, but precarious enough that the psalmist prays, "Do not sweep me away with sinners, nor my life with the bloodthirsty" (v. 9). Is there a sense of being unfairly judged by God? Or are sinners themselves doing the sweeping, taking the psalmist with them along their dangerous and ultimately perishing path?

Regardless, the psalmist proclaims innocence, professes righteousness, and asks for God's vindication. We can imagine David stating his case, saying that he has walked with integrity and "trusted in the LORD without wavering" (v. 1), and praying, "For your steadfast love is before my eyes, and I walk in faithfulness to you" (v. 3). He avoids the worthless, the hypocrites, the evildoers, and the wicked (vv. 4-5). He prays, "O LORD, I love the house in which you dwell, and the place where your glory abides" (v. 8). Because of these things and more David can pray, "Prove me, O LORD, and try me; test my heart and mind" (v. 2), confident that he will pass the test.

The tradition that nurtured me rightly focuses on Paul's words in Romans 3:23—that "all have sinned and fall short of the glory of God." Psalm 26 seems far from this crucial Christian teaching. For many of us it's a foreign, uncomfortable language. Yet like the rest of the psalms, it's God's language because it's God's Word. How do we pray this psalm?

It's important to note that in no place does the psalmist profess to be perfect or without sin. Reading this psalm through the lens of David's life assures us that he had plenty of sin to confess, and various psalms attributed to David include a confession of sin, from Psalm 25 to the familiar and powerful confession of Psalm 51.

Further, like so many psalms, the context of Psalm 26 is one of danger. Some psalms plead for help, others demand help, and still other psalms argue and reason with the Lord for help. A familiar bargaining tool is to say that if something happens to the psalmist, it will reflect badly on God. The pattern in Psalm 26 is to argue that because of righteous living, the psalmist deserves God's help.

Reading Psalm 26 through the lens of David's life, we realize he is not looking for a medal or a seat at God's right hand; he is desperately looking for help and knows that only God can give what he needs.

In the end, this psalm is not primarily about the psalmist's innocence, but about the psalmist's dependence on God. We're given permission in this psalm to make our case before the Lord and to hold nothing back in doing so. The goal, however, is not to prove ourselves right by wrestling a favorable verdict from God's hands. Praying our case is simply another way of naming our dependence on God and desperately seeking God's help.

Woe Is Me! (Ps 31)

The psalmist is either being very dramatic or is in a difficult situation beyond our imagining in Psalm 31. Perhaps an illness is the culprit. As a psalm of David, perhaps we can read this psalm with the story of Absalom in mind (or something similar). One of David's sons, Absalom, rebelled against his father and tried to usurp the throne, but upon his death, David cried, "'O my son, Absalom, my son, my son Absalom! Would I had died instead of you, O Absalom, my son, my son!'" (2 Sam 18:33).

Whatever the context, the psalmist is in a state of misery and has no qualms with letting the Lord know how bad things are: "Be gracious to me, O LORD, for I am in distress; my eye wastes away from grief, my soul and body also. For my life is spent with sorrow, and my years with sighing; my strength fails because of my misery, and my bones waste away" (vv. 9-10). There is no hint of a "grin and bear it" attitude here, nor is there any effort to downplay the pain. This is how the psalmist feels, so this is how the psalmist prays.

To make matters worse, this misery is not confined to private life but extends to all relationships: "I am the scorn of all my adversaries, a horror to my neighbors, an object of dread to my acquaintances; those who see me in the street flee from me" (v. 11). Is there a hint of self-pity or "woe is me" or whining in these words, an exaggeration of the situation in order to evoke pity? If so, it doesn't matter. God can handle our whining just as much as God can handle our anger and our praise. Covenant relationship with God means God wants all of us—the wonderful moments and the whining moments.

It's no surprise that after this description of misery the psalmist says, "But I trust in you, O LORD; I say, 'You are my God'" (v. 14).

It's no surprise that before letting loose with this litany of misery, the psalmist prayed, "Into your hand I commit my spirit" (v. 5). And it's no surprise that toward the end of the psalm, there is either the experience of or the anticipation of relief: "Blessed be the LORD, for he has wondrously shown his steadfast love to me when I was beset as a city under siege" (v. 21).

To pray our misery, even if it may sound like whining to someone else's ears or to our own, is biblical, permissible, and healthy if done faithfully. Faithful whining happens with a trust in and openness to God's presence, an awareness that the Lord listens with steadfast love to complaints that most of us could only tolerate for a few moments. In the course of prayerfully wallowing in our misery, we're given space to express ourselves and work out our misery in a "strong fortress" (v. 2), a safe place where our voice will be heard. It's in the working out of our misery that we come to the place of trust and praise. The situation may or may not have changed, but by the end of our prayer, we can say to ourselves, "Be strong, and let your heart take courage, all you who wait for the LORD" (v. 24).

Praying My Hate (Ps 35)

Do you ever say things when you are angry that you wouldn't normally say in public—words that offend, accusations, curses, labels, or judgments that pour out without the benefit of your usual filters? When we are angry or grieving deeply or feeling threatened, our words often match the vividness of our pain in that moment. The words that erupt might later embarrass us. But ignoring grief, pain, and anger can be far more dangerous than telling the truth.

Imprecatory psalms are psalms that voice Israel's anger and hatred at enemies and the wicked. An *imprecation* is an offensive word or phrase people say when they are angry. Israel's relationship with God was so authentic and so central to the truth of their identity that not only did they speak imprecations to God and about others in prayer, but those prayers became Holy Scripture, recorded forever and offered to God in worship. Sometimes these imprecatory words are a sharp reminder meant to jab God into acting; other times they are an impassioned cry for justice against enemies who currently hold power.

In Psalm 35, a psalm attributed to David, the psalmist wants God "to bring on the adversary dismay commensurate with the trouble the adversary has caused" (Brueggemann and Bellinger,

174). Jesus tells us, "You have heard that it was said, 'An eye for an eye and a tooth for a tooth.' But I say to you, Do not resist an evildoer. But if anyone strikes you on the right cheek, turn the other also" (Matt 5:38-39). Israel, through the lens of David's life, wants an eye and a tooth from the enemy and begs God for all-out resistance to the evildoer.

The fight begins immediately: "Contend, O LORD, with those who contend with me; fight against those who fight against me!" (v. 1). The psalmist wants God to use the weapons of war in the fight: "Draw the spear and javelin against my pursuers" (v. 3). No desire that the enemy might repent and become a friend is expressed. Instead, shame and dishonor are desired for the foe (v. 4). No love or compassion exists for the enemy, only a hunger for the enemy's downfall and destruction: "Let them be like chaff before the wind. . . . Let their way be dark and slippery. . . . Let ruin come on them unawares" (vv. 5, 6, 8).

Throughout the years, Christians have struggled with how to pray, interpret, and simply deal with psalms that call for the judgment or destruction of others. We follow Jesus, the Prince of Peace, who preached a gospel of reconciliation and calls us away from revenge and violence. Unsure of how to approach ancient Israel's imprecations, some church leaders have excised these problematic verses from use in worship. The images are often so violent or shocking that the discomfort they raise in us drives us away from studying or praying through them.

Yet study and pray them we must, for they are part of Jesus' Holy Scripture and ours, along with all other Old Testament texts that seem to lift up or call for violence and destruction. We find guidance in the way Jesus frequently reframed and challenged the understandings of the Torah in his day: "You have heard that it was said, 'You shall love your neighbor and hate your enemy.' But I say to you, Love your enemies and pray for those who persecute you" (Matt 5:43-44). We read the imprecatory psalms through the lens of Jesus' view of the enemy.

Imprecatory psalms like Psalm 35 give us language to pray our hate, but as we pray in Jesus' name, our hate is transformed. Hate unvoiced cannot be dealt with but goes underground, causing all kinds of damage to our hearts and relationships. Psalm 35, prayed in the name of Jesus, reminds us that "the way of prayer is not to cover our own unlovely emotions so that they will appear respectable, but expose them so that they can be enlisted in the work of the kingdom" (Peterson, *Answering God*, 100).

Hate prayed against the perpetrators of injustice becomes advocacy for the victims. It seeks justice for the victims and punishment for the perpetrators, but also prays that the perpetrators will repent and seek to restore what they have broken. Hate prayed against someone who treats us poorly becomes a prayer for strength and wisdom to resist and protect ourselves, but also a prayer for God to soften the heart of the enemy and bring the enemy to repentance. This doesn't feel like "nice" praying, but it is biblically sanctioned. Psalm 35 gives us language to pray our hate so that Jesus can strengthen our love.

Turn Away from Me! (Ps 39)

In a collection of psalms designed to give voice to the vast array of emotions in the human heart, Psalm 39 surprisingly begins with the psalmist trying hard to stay silent. There is fear that to speak will lead to sin, a very real concern when we remember how often our words do harm instead of good. This fear of sin is somehow connected to the presence of wicked people; "I will keep a muzzle on my mouth" (v. 1), presumably because what will be said to the wicked is likely to be sinful.

But something else is going on inside the psalmist. The wicked are not the main problem; God is, which means the urge to speak is too strong, the need to unload and unburden too great: "I was silent and still; I held my peace to no avail; my distress grew worse, my heart became hot within me. While I mused, the fire burned; then I spoke with my tongue" (vv. 2-3). One of the central truths of the psalms still holds true here: what one thinks and feels about God must be voiced to God in prayer.

The psalmist laments how short human life really is: "LORD, let me know my end, and what is the measure of my days; let me know how fleeting my life is" (v. 4). It's not a request for a timetable with the exact date of death so that schedules can be arranged accordingly. Instead, the psalmist wants to live with the awareness that life is short. There is despair in this knowledge, both that life is short by God's design (v. 5, "You have made my days a few handbreaths") and that at times life seems to be meaningless (v. 6, "Surely everyone goes about like a shadow. Surely for nothing they are in turmoil; they heap up, and do not know who will gather").

Yet the voicing of this frustration leads to hope and trust and, ultimately, life: "And now, O LORD, what do I wait for? My hope is in you" (v. 7). As we see so often in the psalms, the speaking of the complaint, the anger, and the frustration is a necessary step in the movement toward trust. To withhold the complaint and state trust alone is to diminish the trust; to speak the complaint and then move to trust is to deepen the trust by making it truly authentic. Further, the arrival at trust includes a dose of humility; human sin plays a role in the fleeting nature of life and its apparent meaninglessness. With the confession "Deliver me from all my transgressions" (v. 8), the psalmist takes some responsibility for humanity's brief lifespan.

Yet there remains another bone to pick. Confession of sin has been made and deliverance from transgressions has been requested, but pardon and forgiveness are in doubt, at least in the psalmist's mind. The psalmist feels oppressed by God: "Remove your stroke from me; I am worn down by the blows of your hand. You chastise mortals in punishment for sin, consuming like a moth what is dear to them" (vv. 10-11). Is God actively striking the psalmist, not with literal, physical blows, but with blows of calamity and distress? Has God's punishment for sin included the taking away of family and possessions, as in the case of Job? Is God's punishment continuing even after confession of sin, with no end of the punishment in sight?

Whatever the answer to these questions, the psalmist both trusts in God (v. 12, "Hear my prayer, O LORD, and give ear to my cry") and seeks relief from God's oppressive presence (v. 13, "Turn your gaze away from me, that I may smile again, before I depart and am no more"). I confess I would like it a lot better if the verses were swapped, with despair expressed first and hope prayed at the end. But despair has the final word, in this psalm at least. Maybe at times that's the best we can do. The situation is so miserable, the grief so unbearable, and the despair so overwhelming that our hope, as real as it is, cannot in that moment override the despair. In its uncomfortable candor Psalm 39 "represents the tension inevitably involved in our response to life . . . both hopeful awe and nearly unspeakable despair that finally cannot be silenced" (Brueggemann and Bellinger, 194) but must be voiced to God, the One who hears and understands.

Life Lessons

I find it much easier to pray "Lead me in your truth, and teach me" (25:5) than "Vindicate me, O LORD, for I have walked in my integrity" (26:1). It feels selfish to whine in prayer and just plain un-Christian to hate in prayer. Thankfully, I've never been in a place where I felt like praying, "Turn your gaze away from me, that I may smile again, before I depart and am no more" (39:13). I suspect I'm not alone in these thoughts.

Many people throughout history and in the present are in difficult and desperate situations, far beyond what I can imagine. It's important for me to get over my discomfort with this language and support sisters and brothers around the world for whom the words of these psalms literally articulate their experience. In doing so, perhaps I—perhaps we—can pray these prayers with and on behalf of those in need. And perhaps we, when the time comes, will be able to pray these words when they do describe our experience.

1. How does God teach you? What helps you maintain openness to God's teaching?

_____
_____
_____
_____
_____

2. What does "waiting on the Lord" mean to you? Do you find such waiting easy, difficult, or somewhere in between?

_____
_____
_____
_____
_____

3. Can you imagine telling God that because of your efforts to walk with integrity and faith that God should rescue you, heal you, deliver you, etc.?

_____
_____
_____
_____
_____

4. What are the positive and negatives of "whining" to a friend when things are not going well? What difference does it make if the recipient of our whining is God?

_____
_____
_____
_____
_____

5. "Enemies," those who victimize innocent people, abound in the world. How does praying our hate for the enemy strengthen our love for and willingness to help the enemy's victims?

6. When we are the enemy's victims, how might God work in us if we pray our hate?

7. Have you ever felt (or known someone who felt) "worn down by the blows of [God's] hand" (39:10)? Does God literally wear us down in present punishment for our sins, or does it just feel that way sometimes? Why?

Thirsting, Praising, Grieving . . . and Angry

Session 4

Book II: Psalms 42–44

Book I ends with three lament psalms (38–40), followed by an individual hymn of thanksgiving and praise. The hymn's final words are a doxology, praising the God of Israel: "Blessed be the LORD, the God of Israel, from everlasting to everlasting. Amen and Amen" (41:13). Immediately, Book II begins with a return to lament, a very real and present part of being human. Just as lament and praise blend in real life, they do so in the psalter as well.

Book II encompasses Psalms 42–72, including eighteen more psalms of David. While David likely wrote a number of these psalms, authorship is a different issue today than it was in ancient Israel. Calling the psalms of Books I and II "Davidic" means that these verses connect to his time period, his life, and the life of Israel during his era. Like Book I, Book II's collection reflects a strong, flourishing Israel under the Davidic monarchy.

Psalms 42–49 are known as the Korahite psalms, hymns and prayers connected to a group of temple keepers and musicians. Korah was a Levite priest who, along with his kindred, was "in charge of the service of song in the house of the LORD," serving as "gatekeepers . . . guardians of the thresholds of the tent" (1 Chron 6:31; 9:19). A "guild of psalmists," the Korahites helped lead Israel's temple services through music and singing (Brueggemann and Bellinger, 204).

Thirsting for God (Pss 42–43)

Many who came through youth group and college in the 1980s and 1990s sang the opening words of Psalm 42 in a popular praise song: "As the deer panteth for the water, so my soul longeth after Thee." The image of being thirsty and longing for water was one we could all identify with, even as well-nourished Americans. We could easily make the move to longing for God, who quenches our thirst both physically and spiritually.

But then the song moved on, borrowing from other psalms and scriptures about the centrality of God in our lives, moving away from the heart of this lament. In many ways, this movement away from lament reflects the spirituality with which many of us were raised: "keep on the sunny side" or the particularly southern "don't air your dirty laundry." Ironically, that sunny/secretive spirituality ignores the reality of lament found in the Psalms and in our lives: "In a society that . . . grows numb by avoidance and denial, it is important to recover and use these psalms that speak the truth about us—in terms of God's engagement with the world" (Brueggemann, *Spirituality*, 13).

Psalm 42 begins with longing and thirsting for God, who seems painfully absent—and might as well *be* absent for the speaker. Any of us who have sensed the absence of God can testify to that feeling of abandonment. We wonder, "When shall I come and behold the face of God?" again (v. 2). In this state, we cannot seem to sense God with us, in corporate worship or in personal prayer, and feel cut off from the water of life (John 4:7-14). Steeped in the living water of the cross and resurrection, we may know in our minds that God does not abandon us, but a downcast heart—thirsty, isolated, and grieving—is rarely comforted by intellectual truths.

The speaker's downcast heart now encounters the water of grief: "my tears have been my food day and night" (v. 3). Sensing a weakened heart, the mockers scoff, "Where is your God?" They imply that if the speaker is truly divinely loved, then such a sense of abandonment could not occur. Surely he must have brought this upon himself, their question suggests.

Mocked and wounded, the speaker calls on the memory of joyfully entering the temple on a festival day (v. 4). In the company of the people of God, the speaker's heart was full of thanksgiving and praise. Now, during a time of turmoil, that remembered joy brings comfort, but only for a moment. Struggling between hope and despair, the psalmist asks, "Why are you cast down, O my soul, and why are you disquieted within me?" Yet then comes the internal answer that sustains: "Hope in God; for I shall again praise him, my help and my God" (v. 5). Shaped by his personal past experience and his people's history, the speaker clings to his only hope: *hope in God.*

Contrary to modern myths about "pulling yourself up by your bootstraps," the speaker knows well that he cannot help himself. The only way to "help himself" is to turn to God, remembering God's goodness in the past and focusing on that goodness as a current and future reality. Like most of us who have suffered deep grief or depression, the psalmist knows he cannot heal his downcast soul.

So the speaker remembers God in the place he finds himself now, near the headwaters of the Jordan River (v. 6; Miller, 839). In this scene, there is not a dearth of water, but excess: "deep calls to deep at the thunder of your cataracts; all your waves and your billows have gone over me" (v. 7). Yet even amidst the overflow of water, hope rises, as God's "steadfast love" keeps the speaker afloat, God's song with him "at night, a prayer to the God of my life" (v. 8; Brueggemann and Bellinger, 205).

Countering the mockers' claim and that of "sunny-side theology," the speaker owns his near drowning in chaos *and* God's song at the same time. Both the struggle and God's song as prayer are true—mutually inclusive. He is not keeping his struggle a secret; he articulates it internally to himself, within his relationship with God and ultimately with the faith community in the form of this psalm. The psalmist places his desperate complaint and plea of forgottenness smack in the middle of his relationship with God. He does not hoard it within, anxiously stewing over what he cannot change. Courageously and vividly, he describes his "deadly wound" and taunting adversaries to the only one with power to change the situation and him (v. 10).

Having once again told his truth in desperate detail, his internal question/answer pattern reemerges: "Why are you cast down, O my soul? . . . Hope in God; for I shall again praise him, my help and my God" (v. 11). Being cast down and disquieted is real and painful and awful. And it is not the last word.

Psalm 43 continues the lament, beginning with a specific petition for vindication. The speaker cannot vindicate himself against "an ungodly people" (v. 1)—that's a God-sized job! The deceitful and unjust are more than the speaker can handle, but not so for the God "in whom I take refuge" (v. 2). Because only God can handle this, the speaker demands to know why God has "cast me off." Why should the ungodly enemy be allowed to oppress and prevail, the speaker asks the God of "light and truth" (v. 5)? What's implied here is that victory of the ungodly is intolerable to a God of justice, a God who has covenanted with Israel.

Finally, led by God's light and truth, the vindicated speaker can return to the temple in joy and worship, praising God "with the harp" (v. 4). Here is the "vow of praise": once restored and delivered, the psalmist will offer praise and thanksgiving to God, sharing the testimony with all who will listen (Brueggemann and Bellinger, 206). With this hopeful image in mind and heart, the speaker offers the question/answer refrain once more: "Why are you cast down, O my soul? . . . Hope in God; for I shall again praise him, my help and my God" (v. 5).

THIRSTY AND HOPEFUL

Upon closer examination, it is clear that Psalms 42–43 are not just about the general human state of longing for God, but about the specific soul-longing we have when sensing God's absence in a time of hurt and trial. This is a cry of *desperate* longing for God, when "tears have been my [our] food day and night" and pain alienates us from others (42:3). With the psalmist we can claim both our downcast soul and our hope that our struggle is not God's last word on us or on the situation. In fact, claiming our struggle and hope together "can lead to maturity" and a deeper faith (Brueggemann and Bellinger, 207). Pretending everything is "fine" or keeping our lament secret will not bless us. As the old adage goes, "Deal with your pain, or your pain will deal with you."

Lament coupled with hope in God bolsters and informs the present and points us toward a brighter future. One day, with the psalmist, we will share the story of our wounding, our prayers, and God's loving response. We will offer up our experience as a witness to the God who has covenanted to be our God "from everlasting to everlasting" (41:13).

Angry at God?!: A National Lament and Plea (Ps 44)

After the internal lament of Psalms 42–43 comes a communal lament, juxtaposing the personal struggle and corporate struggle. Psalm 44 records a national lament, voiced on behalf of the people of God who find themselves in a painful place and look to God for the way out. Many of us who have known the pain of defeat will hear ourselves in these words.

The psalm begins with a testimony of history, celebrating God's powerful intervention in the life of the people (vv. 1-3). Remembering history has always been key to Israel's identity. The retelling of their faith story, from the call of Abraham to the exodus to the prophets, has been essential in their worship. Here, the speakers claim the receipt of that history, in which God "planted" the people in the promised land, won "victory" against their enemies, and delighted in them (vv. 2-3).

The switch to first person in verses 4-7 suggests the speaker is a representative of the people, likely a temple leader, priest, or king (Miller, 840). The representative affirms God's help and salvation against every foe, declaring that Israel's military might was not the cause for the victories (vv. 6-7). In response, the people have fulfilled their vow of praise, boasting and giving thanks to God (v. 8).

Now comes the complaint, served with a daring dose of protest and vivid language. The "yet" of verse 9 contrasts God's past faithfulness with the current reality: God has "rejected and abased us . . . made us turn back from the foe . . . made us like sheep for slaughter" (vv. 9-11). In other words, Israel has been defeated, and it is God's fault. The defeat is not the fault of the military, nor is it due to the enemies' greater might. No, just as God was responsible for the victories, God is now responsible for this defeat (Brueggemann and Bellinger, 209).

It is a *bitter* defeat, captured by the sense that God has "sold your people for a trifle" (v. 12), making them an object of derision and scorn (v. 13). It is as if God has sold them into slavery, having practically given them away to their enemies (Miller, 840). No longer known as God's beloved, protected and prevailing, Israel has become a "byword" or proverbial saying for defeat (v. 14; Miller, 840).

The first person is again used in verses 15-16 as the representative names for the people: "all day long my disgrace is before me, and shame has covered my face . . . at the sight of the enemy and avenger." The people are shamed in front of their foes, defeated and helpless. Their only explanation is that Yahweh has failed them and "abandoned Israel in its time of need" (Brueggemann and Bellinger, 210).

A Faulty Memory?

Though disgraced, the people proclaim their innocence and accuse God of turning against them. They claim not to have forgotten God, having honored the covenant (v. 17) and the first commandment (v. 20; Brueggemann and Bellinger, 210). Instead, God has forgotten them. This accusation is both heartfelt and honest *and* remarkably ironic, calling to mind the countless times God stood by Israel even when Israel turned against God. The book of Judges records this recurring pattern. Israel would do "evil in the sight of the Lord," usually breaking the covenant by worshiping other gods. In angry response, God "sold them into the power of their enemies all around . . . and they were in great distress" (Judg 2:11-23). But God did not forget or abandon the people for long. Each time, God heard their "groaning" (Judg 2:18) and raised up "judges who delivered them out of the power of those who plundered them" (Judg 2:17). Safe and restored again, the people soon "lusted after other gods. . . . They would not drop any of their . . . stubborn ways" (Judg 2:17, 19). So God's anger was rekindled, and the cycle continued. Throughout their history, God remembers and Israel forgets.

But the people protest in Psalm 44: "We have not forgotten you, or been false to your covenant. . . . Our heart has not turned back . . . yet you have . . . covered us with deep darkness" (vv. 17-19). They even remind God that if they had strayed, God would know about it (vv. 20-21)! The people speak with the confidence and audacity of one who is loved and will be—*must be*—heard. With the boldest of language, they call God back to the covenant as God has called them back time and again.

Notably, as followers of Jesus who know our capacity for self-deception, modern readers may wonder if the Israelites were quite as blameless as they claim. Their own history suggests otherwise. But Psalm 44 does not address this possibility, offering instead a snapshot of where Israel is at this moment. Even if they are not blameless, God has always answered their cries before, so whether their claims are accurate or not, their prayer for help is loud and clear.

The people even claim that it is *because* of their faithfulness to God that they are being "killed all day long, and accounted as sheep for the slaughter" (v. 22). The subtext here is that since they are attacked because of faithfulness to God, then it is God's honor at stake if they are defeated (Miller, 841). If God does not act to save Israel, the enemies will be proved right in their claim that their gods are more powerful than Israel's God. Quite a clever argument!

Suddenly turning, the people make their petition to the very One they have accused of abandonment. "Rouse yourself!" they cry together, demanding, "Why do you hide your face? Why do you forget?" (vv. 23-24). This time, they testify, it is *God* who forgets.

Without God's remembrance, they "sink down to the dust" (v. 25).

In closing they call again upon their covenant-God: "Rise up, come to our help. Redeem us for the sake of your steadfast love" (v. 26). They have known God's steadfast love before and know that God's love is what makes them a people. Without God's love, they are not only defeated for now, but forever.

The Bottom Line

What a statement of faith that Israel dares to accuse and petition God in the same psalm! Psychologist Harriet Lerner asserts, "It takes courage to know when we are angry and let others hear about it" (9). Quite often, sharing our anger makes us vulnerable—yet it also has the possibility to invite intimacy and understanding, when shared in a trusted relationship.

Underlying the anger and accusations of Psalm 44 is the rock-bottom belief that God will not truly abandon Israel now. Israel is operating under the assumption that only God has saved them in the past and only God can save them now. They poke, prod, accuse, and petition, funneling all their shame, fear, and anger into their relationship with God. That is the only place where such feelings can be transformed into something life-giving.

In essence, Psalm 44 is full of faith: faith that God will not abandon them, faith that Israel's prodding prayer can and will make a difference, faith that God will reverse their defeat. Their anger and accusation point toward hope: "Israel's hope in YHWH (God) is as strong and vigorous as Israel's accusation against YHWH is daring and candid" (Brueggemann and Bellinger, 210). Notably, the final word of the psalm is about God's steadfast love (v. 26), the bottom line of the covenant.

Anger is part of being human and being in relationship. Like thirst tells us we need water, anger tells us something is wrong and needs to be changed (Lerner, 3–4). The needed change may be internal, external, relational, or a combination of all three. In the snapshot of Psalm 44, Israel was clear that something needed to change and that only God could change it.

Anger honestly acknowledged and voiced to God may lead us to a deeper intimacy with God—and a more authentic faith. Hiding our anger drives it underground, where it can become extremely destructive, even cutting us off from God. As scholar FitzSimon Alison observes, atheism is "one way of expressing anger toward

God" and a far more hostile one than expressing anger openly (Lester, 93).

Anger finds a home in the hands of our most capable God. It becomes one moment in a lifetime relationship, rather than *the* moment that defines or weakens the relationship. Sharing our anger with God reflects a deep trust that God does indeed love us steadfastly and seeks to be in authentic relationship with us.

For those of us who are uncomfortable with anger, Israel's pairing of accusation and petition may not sound like a worship-worthy psalm. For those of us who have been taught we can never be angry at God, Psalm 44 offers a challenge to hear *even anger with God* as a means to worship. Our God can handle Israel's anger, as well as yours and mine, transforming it, and us, in the process.

Life Lessons

Psalms 42–44 contain despair, hope, trust, fear, anger, and praise. Reflected in these powerful verses is the belief that God is intimately involved with humanity and we are intimately involved with God and each other. *Nothing* is barred from the psalmists' relationship with God, not even anger at God. This is covenant love.

In these three psalms, the speakers have a keen awareness of their dependence upon God. If the speaker feels forgotten, the obvious response is to pray for God to remember, even to prod God into remembering. If the speaker's soul is cast down, only God can heal that wound, so the despair is turned to God. If the speaker is angry, only God can redeem that anger, so it is given to God. Within the covenant relationship, absolute vulnerability and openness are not only allowed, but required. When we start hiding the truth of our experience from the One who knows the truth far better than we do, we are in trouble. Despair feeds on itself; anger turns corrosive. What better place to tell the truth about ourselves than in prayer to our God, who, through Christ, "was pleased to reconcile to himself all things" (Col 1:20)?

1. When have you thirsted for God? What was happening in your life? How was that thirst quenched?

2. How do past remembrances of God's intervention in your life (or the lives of others) help you during times of turmoil (42:4-8)?

3. How do you respond when you cannot feel God's presence with you? What helps you regain a sense of that presence?

4. What would you say or do for a friend who felt forgotten by God? How could Psalms 42–43 speak to such a situation?

5. When have you felt angry with God? How did you respond to that anger?

6. What were the messages you were taught about anger with other people and with God?

7. How do you think God receives and hears our anger?

Session 5

The Heart of the Matter: Authentic Confession

Book II: Psalm 51

Between Psalms 44 and 51, the psalmists explore a variety of subjects. After Israel's angry lament and plea for help, Psalm 45 offers a poem for a royal wedding. Psalms 46–48 lift up God's defense of Jerusalem and its inhabitants, God's rule over all nations, and the wonder of God's presence in Zion—clear evidence that the anger of Psalm 44 was indeed transformed.

Psalm 49 features a turn in subject, focusing on the wisdom of trusting in God alone and the foolishness of trusting in earthly riches. The theme remains the same, however: God is sovereign, and we depend on God for everything. Fittingly, God speaks in Psalm 50, calling for repentance for human arrogance and reminding that an acceptable sacrifice is "thanksgiving" (v. 14). Thanksgiving and praise build a bulwark against arrogance, inviting humanity to embrace our role as God's children.

Psalm 51 shows what happens when human arrogance runs amok: sin, brokenness, and painful regret. An arrogant heart takes matters into its own hands, doing what seems right to a self-absorbed soul. In disregarding dependence on God, the arrogant heart rejects the covenant with God and with others, harming everyone in the process. The only fitting response in the aftermath is confession.

A Prayer for Cleansing and Pardon

Psalm 51 is the most familiar of the seven penitential psalms (Pss 6; 32; 38; 51; 102; 130; 143), grouped together by the early church for their tone of repentance. In these psalms, the speaker interprets present difficulties as a judgment or discipline from God. The psalmist generally asks for forgiveness and removal of God's judgment. These seven psalms are often used in liturgies of confession, especially during the season of Lent.

King David's Sins

Historically, the people of God have linked the heartfelt confession of Psalm 51 with the events of 2 Samuel 11:1-27, where David takes Bathsheba, commits adultery, and later has her faithful husband Uriah killed. The prophet Nathan then confronts David by telling a parable in 2 Samuel 12:1-14. Only when confronted in the form of a story about another man does David finally confess his sin.

While scholars debate the historical accuracy of the superscription linking Psalm 51 to David's sin against Bathsheba and Uriah, the connection allows the reader to imagine the depth of repentance the speaker experienced (deClaissé-Walford, 79). In 2 Samuel 11–12, David has become the very king Samuel warned the people about when they first began demanding to have an earthly king like other nations. At that time, God tells Samuel to warn the people that an earthly king "will take" what rightly belongs to him, using that phrase six times over (1 Sam 8:10-18). The same Hebrew form of *take* is used when David "takes" Bathsheba in 2 Samuel 11:3-4, though the connection is lost in the English translation. Put simply, David has become the arrogant king who just "takes" things that are not his to take.

In 2 Samuel 11–12, David has forgotten his commitments to faithfully serve God and the people of Israel. He is thinking only of himself. Many of us know the painful moment of self-awareness when we realize we have forgotten who and whose we are, harming ourselves and others in the process. Psalm 51 captures the emotions, regrets, and hopes of one who is facing such a moment of painful self-awareness.

Words of Confession

The psalmist begins with God's character, making clear his dependence on God's "mercy," "steadfast love," and "abundant mercy" (v. 1). The focus is squarely on God's worthiness and faithfulness. Right from the start, the speaker acknowledges that forgiveness and confession are ultimately about who God is and not who we are. We can only confess our sins because we know that God is merciful and loving, "slow to anger and abounding in steadfast love" (103:8).

Dependent on God's love, the speaker asks God to act: "wash me thoroughly from my iniquity and cleanse me from my sin"

(v. 2). Again, the focus is on God, who will wash and cleanse. The speaker cannot cleanse himself—that is a God-sized job.

Now the speaker is ready to claim the "transgressions" and "sin" that are "ever before me" (v. 3). He cannot wish away or ignore his wrongs; they are right in his face and will not go away. The speaker names his sin against "you, you alone," (v. 4), suggesting "a violation of the first commandment" (Brueggemann and Bellinger, 236).

In the instance of 2 Samuel 11–12, David has placed himself and his own judgment before that of God. He has made an idol of his own human desires. In modern terms, we might call this an abuse of power, a common temptation to use what power God has given us to further ourselves at the expense of others, thus rejecting God's power.

The language "you, you alone" does not necessarily mean "there is no sin against neighbor involved" (Miller, 846). Rather, this language echoes David's simple confession in 2 Samuel 12:13: "I have sinned against the LORD." Sinning against the Lord was the start of David's sin against Bathsheba and Uriah. His first sin was forgetting to have no other gods before God, which led to placing his impulsive desire before the well-being of anyone else. In forgetting God, David forgot himself and his commitment to others.

Fully aware of his sin, the speaker acknowledges that God's sentence and judgment are justified (v. 4). Note that he wastes no time or energy trying to explain away his sin or mitigate the seriousness of his actions—two very real human temptations that get in the way of full, honest confession. The speaker *has seen himself clearly* and is not shying away from what he has done, the only way to confession and forgiveness. In fact, the speaker is so clear about his nature that he proclaims he is a sinner through and through. This is not just a confession of one sin, but an acknowledgement of intrinsic brokenness, something he cannot fix. Like all humans, his "life is permeated with alienation and recalcitrance" (Brueggemann and Bellinger, 236). Thus, he confesses, "I was born guilty, a sinner when my mother conceived me" (v. 5). This is no "woe is me" ploy for leniency, taking guilt to a mawkish extreme. Rather, the speaker is simply naming a clear and obvious reality. He is broken, and only God can heal him.

Having confessed this broken reality to the only One who can heal him and create something new, the speaker turns to what God desires: "truth in the inmost being" (v. 6). Knowing this is beyond his human limitations, he immediately asks God to teach him "wisdom in my secret heart" (Brueggemann and Bellinger, 236). Lying to ourselves is a core component of human sin and brokenness. Telling the truth *about* ourselves *to* ourselves enables us to acknowledge our complete and utter dependence on God. Only as that orientation of God-dependence becomes clear is new life possible.

But in order for God's truth to take root, what is unclean must be removed—again, a God-sized job. So the writer implores God, "Purge me . . . wash me" (v. 7). Purging with hyssop, a bush, was part of an ancient cleansing ceremony (Miller, 847) to make clean what is unclean, such as a home where leprosy has occurred (Lev 14:2-9, 48-53). Here, the speaker invokes the image of that ceremony as he asks to be made clean again. He pleads for a new start that only God can make possible through God's "abundant mercy" and "steadfast love" (v. 1).

Hope for Forgiveness and Healing

With the hope of being washed clean, the speaker can now begin to imagine a new life. His sin has alienated him from God, but confession and forgiveness make possible both reconciliation and a new start. In this new start, "joy and gladness" muted by sin will be heard again, and crushed bones will rejoice (v. 8). All this depends on God's action—hiding God's face from the speaker's sins and blotting out his iniquities (v. 9).

The hope for new life gains another foothold in verse 10. Again, all action is God's: "create in me a clean heart . . . put a new and right spirit within me . . . restore to me the joy of your salvation and sustain in me a willing spirit" (vv. 10, 12). The speaker's awareness of dependence on God's initiative continues. He cannot create a clean heart; he can only confess. He cannot renew his spirit; he can only offer God his broken one. He cannot sustain a willing spirit; he can only ask God to do so. Echoed here is the belief that just as God created in Genesis, God can create a clean heart in this broken sinner. In fact, calling on God as Creator acknowledges that we are God's creatures, fully dependent on God for everything, including—and especially—our renewal. The psalmist trusts that the Creator is still creating.

As Christians, we are also shaped by the apostle Paul's teaching in 2 Corinthians 5:16-21, where anyone who is in Christ is "a new creation, everything old has passed away; see everything has become new! All this is from God." Through Christ, we are all made new.

Through Christ, God is reconciling the world to himself. We who follow Christ are already part of the new creation, being reconciled even as we read these words. The "joy of salvation" (Ps 51:12) is already ours, lived out daily in the process of confession, forgiveness, and reconciliation.

Responding with Praise and Witness

In anticipation of this new creation and joy of salvation, the speaker vows to teach other transgressors God's ways so that they, too, will turn to God (v. 13). His story of new creation will become his witness, teaching others the power of confession, forgiveness, and new life. When God delivers him from bloodshed, he will also "sing aloud of your deliverance" (v. 14). So the expected vow of praise expands with the vow to teach. Just as the speaker's sin has harmed his relationship with God and others, he will now praise God and teach others in response to his own healing. The speaker again asks God to act, even in opening his lips to "declare your praise" (v. 15). He doesn't even pretend to have the capacity to praise without God's help! Because of God's action, the speaker's mouth can praise the One who has ended the alienation created by human sin.

This God-centered, God-enacted praise is what God desires as sacrifice, as named in Psalm 50:14. Burnt offerings are only a "commodity" (Brueggemann and Bellinger, 237), whereas a "broken spirit, a broken and contrite heart" (v. 17) leading to praise are an offering of "the devoted self" that God desires (Brueggemann and Bellinger, 237). A broken spirit and heart reflect a person aware of her need for God, prepared for the new life only God can create. Instead of a prescribed material gift burnt on an altar, God seeks a deeper, more authentic relationship with humanity.

Verses 18-19 may have been a later addition to place sacrifice "in the context of proper worship in the temple and a proper spirit" (Miller, 847). Any offering to God would need to be made with a "broken spirit" of confession and repentance. Burnt offerings offered a means to physically sacrifice part of one's earthly goods as a visible and tangible sign of repentance and restoration of relationship with God. Only when offered with a broken spirit and contrite heart and as evidence of a restored life in God would the temple's tradition of burnt offerings find their proper meaning.

Going through the motions, through burnt offerings or false words, will not work in matters of confession. God will not be fooled. Only a "broken spirit . . . and contrite heart" create circumstances for confession. What good news! *All* we need is a contrite heart.

Once again, the honesty of Psalm 51 flies in the face of any "feel-good Christianity" that insists believers should always feel good and be happy no matter what (a misuse of Paul's call to "rejoice in the Lord always" in Phil 4:4!). In this case, the "feel good" part occurs only after the "feel bad" part when we have to tell the truth about how we have failed God and each other. Contrite hearts and honest confession are not the exception—they are the norm for us.

The Rest of Book II

God's goodness is the greater norm, of course. God hears our confession and forgives, restoring us to new life, just as God hears our laments, holding our pain. We may note that of the twenty-one psalms after Psalm 51 that complete Book II, sixteen are laments. Every lament psalm also includes remembrance of God's past help and/or trust in God's future help, according to God's steadfast love. There is praise within the lament.

However, the praise does not undo the lament or dull the reality of current pain and struggle. Rather, praise and trust remind the speaker that lament will not last forever and is not God's final word. These psalms honor human grief and struggle; they also rest on God's steadfast love, which *will not fail.*

Life Lessons

Psalm 51 moves from deep alienation because of sin to profound joy because of the hope of forgiveness and a renewed relationship with God. Notice that nowhere in the psalm does God or a representative speak a "salvation oracle" that grants forgiveness and offers salvation (Brueggemann and Bellinger, 239). Rather, the joy of restoration is all anticipated. The speaker simply trusts that Israel's covenant-God will once again be faithful to hear his confession, forgive him, and heal the relationship he has damaged.

As followers of Jesus, our trust rests in the life, death, and resurrection of God the Son. The cross and resurrection reflect God the Son's willingness to die and endure separation from God the Father and God the Spirit so that our sins might be forgiven and our brokenness healed. Confession remains an integral part of our relationship with God, but the "assurance of pardon" is never in doubt. This assurance enables us to tell the truth about ourselves to the

One who knows us better than we know ourselves and stands ready to forgive. The empty cross reflects God's continuous offer of forgiveness and new life.

The seriousness of the cross calls us to serious reflection on our sins and brokenness—not with the dread of paralyzing guilt, but the kind of covenant-based honesty that refuses to ignore our wrongs. We've all heard (and given) half-hearted confessions designed to cast blame elsewhere or apologies that carefully avoid any responsibility. Politicians, celebrities, and other public figures have turned this human tendency into a virtual art form.

Psalm 51 invites us into honest confession that tells the truth about ourselves to our loving God. In these verses, God is the one who creates the clean heart, renews the right spirit, and restores the joy of salvation (vv. 10-12): "all that is required is an acknowledgment of need and the psalmist can count fully on God's abiding fidelity" (Brueggemann and Bellinger, 237). God's fidelity allows the speaker to praise and share God's transforming forgiveness with others.

1. Think back to a significant time when you needed God's forgiveness. How did you come to terms with the wrong you had done?

2. What was the experience of confessing like for you? How assured did you feel that God would indeed forgive you?

3. Verses 10-12 put the action in God's hands. Is that part of your experience of forgiveness—that internal changes and spiritual renewal are not ours to create on our own, but God's work? How might this approach make room for real transformation?

4. Is praise an automatic part of your response to forgiveness? How? If not, how might praising God for a past forgiveness bless you now?

5. Have you ever shared a significant experience of forgiveness with someone else? What was that like? If not, would you consider sharing that now?

_____
_____
_____
_____
_____

6. When have you been encouraged by hearing about someone else's experience of forgiveness?

_____
_____
_____
_____
_____

7. What is your response to a clear, honest confession of wrongdoing? To a half-confession that blames others and deflects wrongdoing? When have you seen these two approaches?

_____
_____
_____
_____
_____

8. How might you incorporate Psalm 51 as part of your prayer life when confession is needed? What verses would you pray?

_____
_____
_____
_____
_____

Session 6

Still Praying Even While Everything Falls Apart

Book III: Psalms 73–74, 84, 88–89

Book II of Psalms ends with Psalm 72, a prayer attributed to King Solomon asking God to bless the king, protect the king, and enable the king to rule with justice and mercy. It's a confident psalm prayed with the assurance that God will preserve the Davidic monarchy come what may and, through David's line of kings, keep Israel prosperous. But things do not turn out as Solomon had hoped. Book III, Psalms 73–89, is set against the background of Israel's defeat at the hand of the Assyrians and then the Babylonians, the destruction of the temple, and the end of the Davidic monarchy. The editors choose and arrange psalms that evoke the feelings of despair, longing, and hope that surely occurred among the Israelites during these dark days. They also give us psalms to pray our despair, longing, and hope during the dark days of our lives, when it seems all hope is lost and nothing will ever be the same.

Why Do the Wicked Prosper? (Ps 73)

What happens when the way of the wicked seems to lead not to perishing (1:6), but to prosperity? What happens when the enemy is laughing in triumph and God's laughter at the enemy (2:4) cannot be heard? One possible response is for the righteous to become envious and jealous of the wicked. It's an understandable jealousy when the wicked "have no pain" (v. 4), when "they are not plagued like other people" (v. 5), when "the people turn and praise them" (v. 10), when they are "always at ease" and "they increase in riches" (v. 12).

In contrast, the psalmist's life is most definitely not a bed of roses: "All in vain I have kept my heart clean and washed my hands in innocence. For all day long I have been plagued, and am punished every morning" (vv. 13-14). It's not fair; the one who follows the path of righteousness is seemingly rejected by God, and the ones who flaunt God (v. 11) are experiencing what should be reserved for those who have found favor with God. Have the roles been reversed? Is God now watching over the way of the wicked and ignoring the path of the righteous?

Thankfully, the psalmist is able to resist these jealous thoughts and avoid a fall into the pit of envy. The psalmist is able to say, "But as for me, my feet had almost stumbled; my steps had nearly slipped" (vv. 2-3). Almost stumbled, nearly slipped, but not quite. The jealousy is named—frustration over the injustice of it all is laid out before the Lord in prayer—but ultimately the envy is resisted.

Two things pull the psalmist back from the edge. First, the path of envy will lead the psalmist away from the congregation of God's people and into the camp of the wicked, which is an unthinkable move: "If I had said, 'I will talk on in this way,' I would have been untrue to the circle of your children" (v. 15). The more we focus on the well-being of the wicked and our own comparative suffering, the further we remove ourselves from the community of the righteous, who find strength in each other regardless of circumstances. In that community of relationships with sisters and brothers, there is a relational richness that dwarfs the riches of the wicked.

Step one creates a step back from the pit, but the danger is not over, and the struggle over the success of the wicked is still ongoing: "When I thought how to understand this, it seemed to me a wearisome task" (v. 16). The community is strong, but is it strong enough to sustain the psalmist amid the wicked and their ways? It seemed a wearisome task "until I went into the sanctuary of God; then I perceived their end" (v. 17). The first step is toward the community, the second step is into the sanctuary toward God, and the combination of the two keeps the psalmist from stumbling. God still reigns, the way of the wicked still perishes, and God hasn't left the righteous: "I am continually with you; you hold my right hand" (v. 23).

Because the psalmist has dared to say that the prosperity of the wicked and the suffering of the righteous is unjust, the hand of God now holds the psalmist upright and removes the fear of stumbling. The psalmist does not stand alone, but is surrounded by a community of people whose hands are also held by God. Together, they will resist the temptation of jealousy and will trust in the Lord, each of them able to say with the psalmist, "My flesh and my heart may fail, but God is the strength of my heart and my portion forever" (v. 20).

When we are envious of the success of others, we don't have to hide it from God, but we also don't want to stumble because of it. The praying of our envy exposes its foolishness (vv. 21-22, "When my soul was embittered . . . I was stupid and ignorant") and wakes us up from its folly. In the process of praying our jealousy, we also come to realize how our jealousy is harming our relationship with God: "I was like a brute beast toward you" (v. 22). We enter prayer almost stumbling and nearly falling, but in the praying of our frustration and envy we stay actively engaged with God in such a way that we come to our senses, step back from a fall, and renew our trust in God.

Destruction (Ps 74)

The temple in Jerusalem was the center of Israel's life, the place where sacrifices were offered, prayers lifted up, and songs raised to God. Though not limited to or bound by the temple, the focus of God's presence with Israel was in this magnificent sanctuary built by King Solomon. To say that the destruction of the temple by the Babylonians in 587 BCE was a catastrophic event for Israel would be a vast understatement. It's impossible to fully name how devastating a blow this was to Israel's sense of well-being and identity. But with the help of Psalm 74, it was not impossible for the people to pray how they felt.

"O God, why do you cast us off forever?" (v. 1). The sense of abandonment must be named; there's no getting around the feeling of God's absence. The Lord must be angry with the people to have allowed this to happen: "Why does your anger smoke against the sheep of your pasture?" (v. 1). The prophets had been telling people for years that God's judgment would come if they didn't repent, and following defeat and the exile at Babylonian hands, the prophets would continue to interpret these calamities as punishment for Israel's sin. But right now, in Psalm 74, it's not time to confess, repent, and admit the judgment is justified. Now it's time to pray and ask how God could allow "the sheep of your pasture" to suffer so horribly.

In the aftermath of a tragedy, we often have to rehash and voice the details multiple times as a way of dealing with our shock and pain. Israel engages in this type of therapy, speaking to God like they would speak to someone who has just come on the scene and doesn't know what has happened: "Your foes have roared within your holy place; they set up their emblems there. At the upper entrance they hacked the wooden trellis with axes. And then, with hatchets and hammers, they smashed all its carved work. They set your sanctuary on fire; they desecrated the dwelling place of your name, bringing it to the ground" (vv. 4-7). When the Israelites pray these words, they're not giving God information about the "facts on the ground" as much as they are articulating the ground conditions of their hearts. Describing the devastation was a way of voicing their grief.

Notice the word "your": "your foes . . . your holy place . . . your sanctuary . . . your name." The psalmist articulates Israel's distress but implies that it is God who has been attacked and dishonored. Again, this isn't the time for deep reflection and examination to identify Israel's culpability; it's the time to pray anger and frustration and to argue that God's name is suffering as a result of the calamity. Surely God will want to act to change the situation for God's sake and, as a byproduct, for Israel's sake.

By the end of verse 11, the anger and frustration have been articulated, and the psalmist is ready to praise. The distress is not forgotten; rather, it shapes the praise, and the praise is calculated to move God to action. The praise is no less authentic or faithful simply because it has an ulterior motive. The psalmist (and all who pray this prayer then and now) knows that we bring our whole selves to God when we praise. Our praise is deepened when we name the depth of our distress. It is a sign of deep faith, trust, and dependence when we praise God's power and at the same time ask God to use this power on our behalf.

The litany of praise focuses on God's power in and over creation. In ancient societies, including Israel, the sea was often associated with chaos. Sea monsters symbolized the perils of the deep, dark waters. But the sea's chaos yields to God's order, and the sea's monsters fall by God's hand: "You divided the sea by your might; you broke the heads of dragons in the waters" (v. 13). In the same way, God is able to tame the chaos that engulfs Israel as the temple burns to the ground and is able to crush the enemy with the same power that crushes the sea dragons.

As the creator, God has ownership of creation: "Yours is the day, yours also the night; you established the luminaries and the sun. You have fixed all the bounds of the earth; you made summer and winter" (vv. 16-17). Notice again the use of "yours." This time the focus is not on a building made with human hands (vv. 4, 7, "your holy place . . . your sanctuary"), but on a much larger "building" within which human beings live out their days, that of time itself marked off as day and night. Further, God has created boundaries that limit where human beings can go and what they can do and has established seasons within creation that shape how people live in relation to the created order. The One who established the seasons, fixed the earth's bounds, and to whom day and night belong surely is capable of rescuing Israel from the enemy.

An appeal is made to God's power as creator and then to God's faithfulness as a covenant-maker. "Have regard for your covenant," the psalmist requests (v. 20), acknowledging the covenant God has made with Israel and pleading with God to honor this covenant by rescuing the people. Again, this isn't the time to assess how well or how poorly Israel has kept its part of the deal in their covenant relationship with God. This is a time to cry out in pain and helplessness. The cry of Psalm 74 ultimately is a cry of deep faith, for Israel knows that only God can save them from the destruction. The evidence on the ground is that God has forgotten them or left them or is punishing them, yet "the congregation does not yield its faith to experience but instead shapes its bitter experience into poignant urgent prayer" (Mays, 246).

"Better is one day in your house" (Ps 84)

The destruction of the temple provides the historical background for Book III, yet tucked away in Book III is one of the psalter's greatest celebrations of the temple's glories. Psalm 84 "reflects worship in Jerusalem during the Davidic monarchy" (Brueggemann and Bellinger, 364), when the temple was standing tall at the center of Israel's life and relationship with God. Why was this psalm placed at this point in the psalter, where the editors were giving Israel language to voice their pain and fear and suffering at the hands of the Babylonians?

It could be that the editors were tapping into and affirming Israel's longing for home. Whether prayed while in exile or in Israel several hundred years later when the Romans were in charge and the rebuilt temple was a shadow of its former self, this psalm points to the temple as "home," the place where God dwells. When you were within its walls, all was right with the world for the children of Israel.

While any local church is a living organism centered in a gathered group of believers, the actual buildings of a local church are of vital importance as a place where people gather to meet God. When

I think of the church of my childhood and youth, I remember so many things about the place itself. I can easily picture myself in Mr. Brady's fifth-grade Sunday school class where I learned my first psalm verse. It doesn't take much for me to hear the bounce of the ping-pong ball in the youth room. If I sit still for just a moment and close my eyes, I can smell the turkey and pumpkin pie at our church's annual Thanksgiving dinner. But the room I remember most, the room that shaped me more than any other, is the sanctuary. I remember the people who helped lead worship, the people with whom I worshiped in the pews, being overwhelmed by the bright lights shining in my face as I was baptized. But most of all I remember sensing, feeling, being aware of God's presence. The place, the people, and the purpose of the sanctuary all combined to make me attentive to the holy, aware that I was on holy ground. God is everywhere, of course, but whenever I return to that sanctuary in my mind, I'm coming home to God.

Psalm 84 originally was most likely a pilgrim song, sung when one arrived at the temple. After the temple's destruction, it became a longing-for-home psalm, a way of traveling in the mind to the place of old where the presence of God was found. Naturally, praise of the place itself must be voiced: "How lovely is your dwelling place, O LORD of hosts!" (v. 1). Because it is so lovely, but most of all because God dwells there, the psalmist confesses, "My soul longs, indeed it faints for the courts of the LORD" (v. 2).

Though the psalm is written as a personal prayer, the superscription says it is "of the Korahites," worship leaders during the days of the Davidic monarchy. This is a community prayer, sung in worship by the congregation before it is prayed by individuals alone. Inserted in the text after verses 4 and 8 is the word *Selah*. As to its meaning, "scholars guess 'pause for a benediction,' or 'louder here—fortissimo' . . . *Selah* directed people who were *together* in prayer to do something or other *together*" (Peterson, *Answering God*, 83–84). I have no memory of being alone in my home church sanctuary, though it certainly could have been a place at times during the week where I could have gone to pray in solitude. All of my memories of the place include people: people singing, people praying, people listening to a person preaching during worship; people laughing and smiling and embracing in Jesus' name before and after worship; people crying and grieving and hoping before, during, and after a funeral. Since those days I've found lots of places where I pray alone, but the sanctuary of my home church, like the temple for the people of Israel, remains in my mind a place where I gather with sisters and brothers to worship God.

God and people and place—all three converge at the temple to make it "home" for Israel, so much so that Israel gushes in verse 10, "For a day in your courts is better than a thousand elsewhere. I would rather be a doorkeeper in the house of my God than live in the tents of the wicked." The place and the people in the tents of the wicked lead one far away from God, but the place and the people of the temple do just the opposite. God and people and place, but mostly God. "The experience of the particular place puts the psalmist in touch with God's sovereignty over all places" (McCann, 1013), so in the remembering of a particular place of worship, we are ultimately drawn not to the place but to God. Longing for the place is just one small facet of our larger longing for God, which is why this wonderful celebration of the temple ends pointing us not to the temple as home, but to God as home: "O LORD of hosts, happy is everyone who trusts in you" (v. 12).

Rock Bottom, but Still Praying (Ps 88)

Since the historical backdrop for Book III is the destruction of the temple and the end of the Davidic monarchy, it's not surprising that a deep lament psalm is placed in this part of the psalter. What sets Psalm 88 apart from all the other lament psalms is the absence of praise and explicit statements of trust. There is no movement from despair to hope or from complaint to faith. The psalmist is down in the dumps as the psalm begins and remains in the dumps when the psalm ends. The voicing of the despair creates no mood shifts and does not strengthen faith or generate hope.

The specifics of the situation are not mentioned, only that the psalmist is close to death: "For my soul is full of troubles, and my life draws near to Sheol" (v. 3). *Sheol* is the Old Testament word for the place of the dead and is often referred to as "the Pit" (v. 4). "In Sheol, people existed as 'shades' in a world of misery and futility" (Rainwater, 819), which is why the psalmist asks God in verse 10, "Do the shades rise up to praise you?" The logic of the appeal is that unless God saves the psalmist from death, the psalmist will no longer be able to offer praise and give testimony to the steadfast love of the Lord in the land of the living. In other words the psalmist seems to be asking, "Do you really want to lose a voice that praises you?"

Whatever the cause of this suffering leading unto death, the psalmist interprets it as coming from the hand of God. The distress is due to God's intentional action: "You have put me in the depths of the Pit" (v. 6). God's action flows from anger and is not meant to be subtle: "Your wrath lies heavy upon me, and you overwhelm me with your waves" (v. 7). To make things even worse, God designs the distress so that the psalmist experiences it alone: "You have caused my companions to shun me; you have made me a thing of horror to them" (v. 8).

At the point of death, overwhelmed by the wrath of God, and all alone by divine intent, why does the psalmist not curse God and hope to die? Why not move from "O LORD, why do you cast me off?" (v. 14) to "I'm done with God"? The psalmist doesn't tell us why, but my guess is the thought of walking away from God was never an option. This psalmist, and the Israelites in general, were so immersed in a personal, covenant relationship with God that they would rather be angry at God than give up on God.

When we arrive at the last verse, there has been no change in the psalmist's despondent tone: "You have caused friend and neighbor to shun me; my companions are in darkness" (v. 18). But the psalmist is still praying, still pleading, still able to say, "But I, O LORD, cry out to you; in the morning my prayer comes before you" (v. 13). The prayer itself, though the despondency never lifts, is evidence of faith and trust and an absolute dependence on God.

In his novel *The Night Train*, Clyde Edgerton describes a conversation between Ted Stephens, a white pastor, and Isaac Wilson, a black pastor, in 1960s North Carolina, in which Ted "confided that he was friends with an atheist. Ted never forgot what Isaac said: None of my people can afford to be atheists" (Edgerton, 28). And so it was for Israel, even when it seemed that they had been completely abandoned by God.

End of the Promise? (Ps 89)

The second psalm of Book III, Psalm 74, describes the destruction of the temple in Jerusalem by the Babylonians. The last psalm of Book III, Psalm 89, describes the end of the Davidic dynasty that accompanied this military defeat. For 400 years an ancestor of David had occupied the throne in Israel. Now, there is no temple and no king. In Book IV, the editors will bring us psalms that focus on God as king, thus shifting Israel's hope away from an earthly king and centering their trust in the Lord. But before doing so, the end of David's reign must be lamented, and Israel's bewilderment must be voiced.

The first eighteen verses of Psalm 89 quickly move us away from the despondency of Psalm 88. Israel is praising God once again. The praise, though, aims toward one specific act of God: "You said, 'I have made a covenant with my chosen one, I have sworn to my servant David: "I will establish your descendants forever, and build your throne for all generations"'" (vv. 3-4).

Verses 19-37 list the promises God made to David, including an astounding promise in light of the failure of David's descendants to walk closely with God: "I will establish his line forever, and his throne as long as the heavens endure. If his children forsake my law and do not walk according to my ordinances, if they violate my statutes and do not keep my commandments, then I will punish their transgression with the rod and their iniquity with scourges; but I will not remove my steadfast love, or be false to my faithfulness. I will not violate my covenant, or alter the word that went forth from my lips" (vv. 29-34).

Of course, David's descendants did forsake God's Law in ridiculously repetitive fashion and often showed no interest in keeping God's commandments. The rod and the scourges of God's punishment were applied by the Babylonians, according to the prophets. Some parts of the promise remain intact; Israel and its Davidic kings did not walk according to God's ordinances, and now they have been punished. But the crucial promise—that a king from David's line would remain on the throne forever—appears broken, as there is now no king at all. It feels like God's steadfast love has been removed.

All that's left for Israel to do is plead with the Lord, which happens in verses 46-51. David asks the "How long?" question in Psalm 13; now it's as if all of Israel is asking, "How long, O LORD? Will you hide yourself forever?" (v. 46).

Life Lessons

The destruction of the temple in Jerusalem by the Babylonians in 587 BCE is one of the main pivot points in the Old Testament. "Major" prophets like Isaiah, Jeremiah, and Ezekiel, along with "minor" prophets like Amos and Haggai, all either warned Israel that judgment was coming if the people did not repent or spoke a prophetic word of hope and challenge during and after the exile that followed defeat. Book III brings us into the depth of Israel's pain and bewilderment over the temple's destruction and the end of David's royal line of kings.

Eventually, the longing for the revival of David's line would shift to longing for God's promised messiah to come. The events described in the psalms of Book III are part of the seedbed of Israel's messianic hope. Jesus, born of David's family tree (Matt 1:6, Luke 3:31), would fulfill that promise in ways Israel did not expect, coming as a suffering servant and not as the conquering king.

But before Israel could start longing for the messiah, the people needed to mourn the failure of the Davidic monarchy and name their sense of abandonment: "LORD, where is your steadfast love of old, which by your faithfulness you swore to David?" (v. 49). We, too, need to stay with them in their pain as we read these psalms and not jump too quickly to the good that God will bring from this crisis when Jesus is born.

In the same way, when tragedy occurs in our lives or in the life of someone we know, we need to stay with the pain. Though we may have a great assurance of God's presence in the moment and though we may have great hope that out of the ashes God can bring good, that assurance and hope does not negate or diminish the pain. As we've seen in psalm after psalm, the pain and despair must be expressed. The expression of pain in prayer is a sign of faith and forms an openness to the One who weeps with us and holds us in our pain.

1. In what ways are you jealous of the wicked? When/if you stumble because of this jealousy, what does it look like?

2. When and how has your church family kept you from stumbling? When and how has God gotten your attention in a worship service and put you back on the right path?

3. Sit with the Israelites for a moment as they mourn the destruction of the temple. What was life like for them in that moment?

4. Is there (or has there been) a church sanctuary where you sense and feel God's presence? Why?

5. How can the very act of praying even when full of doubt and devoid of stated trust still be an act of faith? Have you ever prayed your doubts?

_____
_____
_____
_____
_____

6. Why is it so tempting when we're comforting others to try to find some "silver lining" in their pain? Why is it so hard to stay with people in their pain?

_____
_____
_____
_____
_____

Session 7

Turning to God as King
Book IV: Psalms 90, 95, 103, 105–106

Book III ends with the Davidic dynasty no more, the temple destroyed by the Babylonians, and the best and brightest of Israelite society marched off into exile. But a corner is turned in Psalm 90. Exile does not have the final word; there is hope for the people of Israel. The editors of the book of Psalms knew that "the only hope of survival in these bewildering circumstances is for the people to go back—to remember—a time in their past when God, not an earthly king, was sovereign over them" (deClaissé-Walford, 99). So they chose a psalm ascribed to Moses, made it Psalm 90, then sprinkled Book IV (Pss 90–106) with psalms that make reference to Moses and his era, all as a way of shifting the people's hopes from a human king to God as king. Only when they embrace God's rule over them will they find strength in the time of struggle, and only God their king can bring victory out of their defeat.

Approaching the King (Ps 90)

Getting clear on the fact that God is God and the people are not is a crucial first step in the embrace of God as king. The psalmist accomplishes this by contrasting God's eternal nature to humanity's fleeting nature: "For a thousand years in your sight are like yesterday when it is past" (v. 4), but for human beings the "days of our life are seventy years, or perhaps eighty, if we are strong" (v. 10). This reminder does not produce paralyzed resignation to our human fate, nor does it ignite a hyperactive effort to get things done because the time is short. Instead, it calls us to receive each day as a gift from God our king, under whose reign we seek to live, doing each day's work in its time, loving God, and loving people in each moment. Before the Eternal One a finite mortal petitions, "So teach us to count our days that we may gain a wise heart. . . . Satisfy us in the morning with your steadfast love, so that we may rejoice and be glad all our days" (vv. 12, 14).

But this divine ruler has expectations and is no stranger to anger when those expectations are not met. Surely the editors heard echoes of God's present judgment in the divine anger experienced by Israel in Moses' day: "For we are consumed by your anger; by your wrath we are overwhelmed. . . . Who considers the power of your anger? Your wrath is as great as the fear that is due you" (vv. 7, 11).

Israel's divine king is no docile, disengaged, do-what-you-want-it's-okay-with-me kind of ruler, but a fully alert and attentive sovereign who demands love, loyalty, and justice. Where these demands are not met, the wrath of God is activated and comes on the scene. But God's wrath is not irrational, unrestrained, or out of control. God can turn from anger, even at the urging of a human being. Exodus 32, where Moses pleads with God to relent and not destroy the people in anger, and Psalm 90:13 are the only two places in the Old Testament where we see "a human being admonish God to turn . . . and change God's mind" (deClaissé-Walford, 104). The bold cry of "Turn, O LORD! How long? Have compassion on your servants!" (v. 13) then leads to an unashamed, unembarrassed, and unhesitating request for God's blessing: "Let the favor of the Lord our God be upon us, and prosper for us the work of our hands— O prosper the work of our hands!" (v. 17).

The Eternal King, the One who "from everlasting to everlasting" (v. 2) is God, is also the approachable king. The One who makes clear and non-negotiable demands for obedience and gets angry when those demands are not met is also the One who satisfies us with steadfast love, makes us glad, teaches us to count our days, and prospers the work of our hands. To this king Israel is called to turn in the traumatic, difficult days of the exile. And to this king, whose character and love were fully revealed to us in the life, death, and resurrection of Jesus, we are called to devote our lives.

O Come Let Us Worship . . . and Obey (Ps 95)

It was early July, hot and muggy in southeastern Virginia. We were sweaty, thirsty, and cranky as we walked the streets of Colonial Williamsburg with our boys, ages ten, eight, and six at the time. Lunch was just around the corner, we kept saying; we were almost there. But when we turned the corner, we saw a huge throng of people, gathered at the base of a tall building, with several actors in period costume standing on a balcony and speaking to the crowd. One of them pulled out a long scroll-like paper, saying, "We hold these truths to be self-evident," and, with the other actors, proceeded to read the Declaration of Independence in its entirety.

I'd like to say our boys were mesmerized and bombarded me with questions about our nation's history once the declaration had been read. Instead, we moved as quickly as we could to the restaurant in order to beat the crowd, but for a brief moment we participated in an important national ritual that occurs every year around the Fourth of July. The reading of the Declaration of Independence on that hot July day was more than a remembering of our national founding; it was an annual reenactment and reminder of our nation's birth.

In similar fashion it is believed that Israel had an annual enthronement festival to reenact God's enthronement as king, a festival that not only reminded Israel that God is king, but renewed Israel's commitment to follow and serve the Lord. Psalm 93 and Psalms 95–99 are called *enthronement psalms*, most likely read, recited, and sung at these annual festivals.

It is easy to imagine the Israelites singing Psalm 95 at an annual festival because we sing or say these words in worship so often: "O come, let us worship and bow down, let us kneel before the LORD, our Maker! For he is our God, and we are the people of his pasture, and the sheep of his hand" (v. 6). Verses 1-7a are familiar liturgical language, used both for worship in the gathered community and in personal prayer.

Verses 7b through 11 are not familiar, rarely said or sung in worship or prayed in private. They shift from the comfortable language of praise to the uncomfortable voice of warning. Literally, the voice shifts as well, from Israel singing praise to God directly speaking warning: "Do not harden your hearts, as at Meribah, as on the day at Massah in the wilderness, when your ancestors tested me, and put me to the proof, though they had seen my work" (vv. 8-9).

In the wilderness the people were thirsty, accusing Moses and by implication God of bringing them out of Egypt in order to die of thirst. God had provided manna from heaven each day, so why should they doubt that God would provide water to quench their thirst? God does not chastise them, but provides water from the rock when Moses hits it with his staff, and the place was given the names Massah and Meribah (Exod 17:1-7). God provides but still says of Moses' generation, "They are a people whose hearts go astray, and they do not regard my ways" (v. 10).

We skip verses 7b-11 for the logical reason that we'd rather sing God's praises than hear God's warnings. We'd rather praise God as king than listen to God as judge. But both voices are necessary, in corporate worship and private prayer. The king who calls forth our praise also demands our obedience, in ancient Israel and today.

The Steadfast Love of God, Our King (Ps 103)

It was a beautiful spring evening. A nice breeze was blowing, the sun was setting, and a few clouds were moving across a deep blue sky. So I did what human beings have been doing for thousands of years; I stopped what I was doing, gazed upward, and savored the view.

But something happened in my gazing that's only happened for the last 100 years or so. A plane flew into view, slowly making its way across the sky, a line of exhaust trailing behind it, the sun shining on it. When David looked up at the sky for an evening sunset in ancient Israel, when Hannah the mother of Samuel gazed up at the sky, they never saw an airplane.

That we can fly above the clouds and send people into space shapes the way we read Psalm 103:11: "For as the heavens are high above the earth, so great is his steadfast love toward those who fear him." We focus on a long distance we have spanned, so we rightly understand verse 11 to mean as great as the distance is to the clouds, so great is God's love and faithfulness toward us.

The same would have been true for Hannah and David and their fellow Israelites, but this verse would have meant much more. They would likely have interpreted these words literally, believing that God's love literally reaches from earth as high as the heavens and is literally present everywhere in between. In other words, God's steadfast love permeates all of creation and is inescapable. God's steadfast love and faithfulness are the fundamental, defining, ultimate realities in the world; we really do live and move and have our being in the presence of God.

What are the "benefits" (v. 2) of living in tune with this ultimate reality? Forgiveness is at the top of the list. The Lord "forgives all your iniquity. . . . He does not deal with us according to our sins, nor repay us according to our iniquities. . . . As far as the east is from the west, so far he removes our transgressions from us" (vv. 3, 10, 12). As Israel comes to terms with the fact that defeat and the exile were the consequences of their sins, it must have felt like a huge burden was lifted from their shoulders to hear of God's incredible forgiveness in Psalm 103. To those of us who know how much our transgressions hurt other people, prevent us from being all that God wants us to be, and how much sin weakens God's work through us, the same message of forgiveness in Psalm 103 sets us free to love God, others, and ourselves.

God can be so incredibly forgiving because "the LORD is merciful and gracious, slow to anger and abounding in steadfast love" (v. 8). In one sense this is a statement of faith: We believe God to be merciful and gracious. It is also a theological statement describing what God is like—"slow to anger and abounding in steadfast love"—that then helps us explain what God does—"forgives all your iniquity" (v. 3).

But this is not a verse simply to be dissected in a seminary classroom or in Sunday school. This is a verse that makes our hearts sing! We say it not to explain God, but to praise God! It's a verse to pray over and over as a way of moving its truths from our heads to our hearts.

Notice that this verse so full of mercy, grace, and steadfast love also includes anger. The psalmist does not say God never gets angry, but says God is slow to anger. Israel is very familiar with God's anger, with Book III having portrayed defeat at the hands of the Babylonians and Book IV portraying life in exile, both of which occur because of God's anger over Israel's sins. So it would not be surprising if the Israelites in exile were to "presume that the divine anger will endure, but Psalm 103 intones a different and surprising way of God in the world" (Brueggemann and Bellinger, 443).

A 1970s television show brought to the screen a comic book character known as the Incredible Hulk. Because of an accidental radiation overdose in a scientific experiment, David Banner's body chemistry is gruesomely transformed so that when he becomes angry, his skin turns green, his muscles expand, and he becomes a roaring creature with incredible strength that leaves behind a path of destruction. To an investigative reporter who is pressing him just a little too much with his questions, Banner says, "Please don't make me angry. You wouldn't like me when I'm angry."

Thankfully, it is not the case that God's anger builds and builds until it explodes in fury. With this phrase, "slow to anger," Israel is able to say that God's anger is always purposeful, never out of control, and always in service to God's steadfast love.

With this psalm Israel reinterprets its defeat; God's anger and judgment on David's dynasty do not mean God's steadfast love for Israel has ended. By looking back to a time before David, when the Lord "made known his ways to Moses, his acts to the people of Israel" (v. 7), Israel refocuses on God's sovereignty over all creation: "The LORD has established his throne in the heavens, and his kingdom rules over all" (v. 19). In this new and difficult political reality, God still rules, though it may not seem so on the surface. Beneath the surface, however, the steadfast love of the Lord sustains the people and gives them strength. Through the voice of the psalmist, Israel can say, "Bless the LORD, O my soul, and all that is within me bless his holy name" (v. 1).

Remembering Times of Faith and Times of Sin (Pss 105–106)

Our church has a tradition of recognizing at homecoming every year those who have entered their fiftieth year as members of the church. An interview is recorded with each person as they share their memories of the past fifty years, and that interview is shown during the homecoming service. Every year, the same person's name comes up as these fifty-year members recall how they came to our church: "old man Baker." Back then, "old man Baker" would visit every family that moved into the neighborhood surrounding the church and invite them to attend our worship service. His trademark was a pocket-knife that he used to knock on people's doors; people remember the knock, they remember the non-negotiable quality of the invitation (!), but most of all they remember Mr. Baker's commitment to God and to our church and the way this commitment produced care and concern for their lives.

Mr. Baker died many years ago, but we still have the pocketknife he used to knock on doors; it is a treasured artifact of our church's history. More importantly, we have the stories and the memory of his acts of witness and service. Fifty-year members tell the stories every year because Mr. Baker's story was a significant part of their life story. But on the annual occasion of sharing Mr. Baker stories, our church is being shaped for present and future ministry. Times are different now, and an old man knocking on doors with a pocket-knife in our church's neighborhood would not go over well. But people all around us still hunger for relationship, and God still calls us to reach out to them with the love of Jesus. In the spirit of "old man Baker's" outreach, God continues to send us out to love our neighbors.

Psalm 105 is a celebration of what God has done in Israel's history through the lives of several individuals. Israel's history started with Abraham, Isaac, and Jacob, and the covenant God made with them still stands: "He is mindful of his covenant forever . . . the covenant he made with Abraham, his sworn promise to Isaac, which he confirmed to Jacob as a statute" (vv. 8-10). When famine struck the land, God provided for Israel by placing Joseph in a position of power in Egypt, where he could provide food for his people (vv. 16-25). When the people cried out generations later because they were enslaved by Pharaoh, God sent Moses and Aaron to lead the exodus out of Egypt (vv. 26-36). And in their journey through the wilderness and into the promised land, God provided for the people's every need (vv. 37-44).

This retelling of the story has a homecoming-like feel. The celebration of God's work through these individuals is set in the context of worship, with a focus on thanksgiving and praise for all that God has done: "O give thanks to the LORD, call on his name, make known his deeds among the peoples. Sing to him, sing praises to him; tell of all his wonderful works" (vv. 1-2). A central aspect of worship in any age is recounting all that God has done in the past; as followers of Jesus, in our worship we tell of God's work in Israel, and we tell over and over again the story of Jesus' life, death, and resurrection. We are giving thanks to God and praising God as we do so.

But worship also shapes us in the present. Remembering what God has done in the past through our ancestors forms us to be people through whom God can work now. Psalm 105 takes a long walk through the history of Israel and at the end of the journey, in the very last verse, explains why the journey was taken in the first place: "that they might keep his statutes and observe his laws" (v. 45). Through people like Abraham, Isaac, Jacob, Joseph, and Moses, the "sovereign of the universe sought to establish a colony of obedience, an enclave of those who represented and displayed his reign" (Mays, 339), a people through whom God could bless the world (Gen 12:3). Every time Israel recounts its history by reciting Psalm 105, the call to obedience is renewed. Every time we worship, telling the stories of Jesus and the stories of ancestors in the faith like "old man Baker," the call to obedience and to a life of sacrificial service and witness to the neighbor is put before us once again, awaiting our response.

Psalm 106 recounts Israel's history as well, but with a different twist. It's the same history, but a different part of the story is emphasized: Israel's sin. In Egypt, God did miracles for Israel, but the people did not always respond faithfully: "Our ancestors, when they were in Egypt, did not consider your works" (v. 7). God parted the waters, the Israelites walked through on dry land, Pharaoh's army drowned when the waters covered them, and the people believed God's "words; they sang his praise. But they soon forgot his works . . . and put God to the test in the desert" (vv. 12-14). The people "made a calf at Horeb and worshiped a cast image. . . . They forgot God, their Savior, who had done great things in Egypt" (vv. 19, 21).

Over and over again, Psalm 106 recounts the people's faithlessness and God's punishment, but most of all God's patience. Now, as the editors place Psalm 106 into the collection of psalms, the Israelites are in another crisis due to their sin, with the Davidic monarchy no more, the temple a shadow of its former self, and many of the people still dispersed because of the cataclysmic events that occurred hundreds of years earlier when the Babylonians destroyed Jerusalem. Having confessed the sin of their ancestors and their own sin through the praying of this psalm, the psalm moves toward its conclusion with the prayer, "Save us, O LORD our God, and gather us from among the nations, that we may give thanks to your holy name and glory in your praise" (v. 47).

We don't have a homecoming tradition at our church where we remember and publicly name our church's sins in the past. I suspect your church is like ours in celebrating stories of faithfulness but neglecting stories of sin. I'm certainly not suggesting that the sins of individuals from the past should be announced from the pulpit, but I wonder what it would look like if predominantly white churches would repent of their past racial prejudices as they remembered their history. I wonder what it would look like if wealthy churches confessed the times when their wealth was not used wisely to bless a world in need, but was used selfishly to maintain a sense of status and comfort. I suspect such confessions would cause people to confess their sins and lead their churches to work toward racial reconciliation in their communities and use more of their resources to empower those who are under-resourced.

Psalms 105 and 106 go together in Israel's praying and in our praying, exposing our sinfulness and exalting God's graciousness: "Psalm 105 makes the people's faithlessness look all the more grievous. . . . Psalm 106 makes God's grace look all the more amazing" (McCann, 1104). Psalm 105 gives Israel examples to follow of trees planted by streams of water, but most of all points them to God's grace and power. Psalm 106 keeps Israel honest and humble, confessing sin and depending on God's forgiveness. And through our praying of both psalms, whether at homecoming or any time of year, we give thanks for God's work in the past, confess our sins past and present, and acknowledge our dependence on God both now and in the future.

Life Lessons

The psalms considered in this section have a wonderful resonance with the Lord's Prayer. One way to pray the Lord's Prayer is to pause after each line and pray a thought or request that the phrase triggers in our hearts. In this way the Lord's Prayer can be prayed in conjunction with the psalms.

We pray "Our Father," and Psalm 103:13 helps describe the phrase: "As a father has compassion for his children, so the LORD has compassion for those who fear him."

To pray "Our Father, who art in heaven" is to say that God transcends life and time as we know it: "Before the mountains were brought forth, or ever you had formed the earth and the world, from everlasting to everlasting you are God" (90:2).

To hallow God's name is to praise God, something Psalm 95:6 calls us to do: "O come, let us worship and bow down, let us kneel before the LORD, our Maker!"

As Israel turns its attention in Book IV to a time when God was their only king, they foreshadow the prayer "Thy kingdom come, thy will be done on earth as it is in heaven." We can pray the phrase with Psalm 103:6 in mind: "The LORD works vindication and justice for all who are oppressed." Wherever there is injustice, suffering, and strife, we pray for God's kingdom to come and God's will to be done in that place as it is in heaven (for example, "Thy kingdom come, thy will be done, in the Middle East as it is in heaven").

When we pray "Give us this day our daily bread," we're reminded that every day is a gift from God and that no day can be lived apart from God's provisions. Psalm 90:12 has taught us a similar lesson: "So teach us to count our days that we may gain a wise heart."

To pray "Forgive us our trespasses as we forgive those who trespass against us" is to call to mind the beautiful truth that "the LORD is merciful and gracious, slow to anger and abounding in steadfast love" (103:8).

Voicing the request "And lead us not into temptation but deliver us from evil" puts us in the company of the Israelites who cried, "Save us, O LORD our God, and gather us from among the nations" (106:47).

Praying "for Thine is the kingdom and the power and the glory, forever" brings us to the end of Book IV as we pray, "Blessed be the LORD, the God of Israel, from everlasting to everlasting. And let all the people say, 'Amen.' Praise the LORD!" (106:48).

1. How does counting our days help us receive each day as a gift?

2. What does it mean for you to think of God as "king"?

3. How would our worship services be impacted if we prayed the warning verses of Psalm 95 as well as the familiar verses of praise?

4. Accepting with our minds that Jesus forgives our sins is often easier than accepting this truth in our hearts. What do the words "as far as the east is from the west, so far he removes our transgressions from us" (103:12) say to your heart?

5. How does the phrase "slow to anger" shape your understanding of God's anger?

6. Who are the people in your church's history that have helped your church serve God faithfully? If they are still living, how are they thanked for their faithfulness? If they are no longer with us, how is their memory kept alive to inspire current and future generations?

7. How can churches name, confess, and repent of past sins?

8. Experiment with praying a different psalm verse with each phrase of the Lord's Prayer. Describe your experience.

Session 8

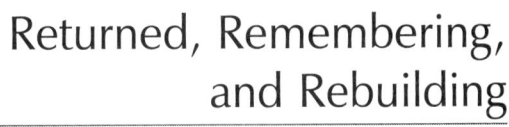

Returned, Remembering, and Rebuilding

Book V: Psalms 107–119

Have you ever used the memory of a favorite song or happy occasion to help in the midst of a difficult time? I come from a singing family, so when I feel down, I often find that my grandmother's best-loved hymns comfort me. Some of us keep memories of family highlights stored in our hearts for times when we need encouragement or reassurance. Drawing on our past is key for navigating the present.

The Israelites draw on their past throughout Book V. Hope from former days and the accompanying psalms buoy the Israelites as they navigate an uncertain future. They call on the best of days gone by to remind them of who and whose they are, even as they interpret a very changed present.

Psalms 107–150 make up this last book of the Psalms, set in the period after the exile. Having defeated the Babylonians, the Persians send the exiled Israelites back home over a period of years. But what they return to is not the home they knew: the temple is in ruins, Jerusalem is a shadow of its former glory, and they are no longer an independent kingdom but subjects of Persia. Just as the exile forced the Israelites into a critical time of self-examination and theological rethinking, so does the postexilic period. The psalms of Book V give us a glimpse into that process.

The Return of the King

Notably, King David reappears in these psalms. In Books I and II, the Davidic kingship is a key focus culturally and theologically. But with defeat by the Babylonians, which felled the southern kingdom of Judah, David's dynasty is no more. Fittingly, the focus shifts in Books III and IV to lamenting that loss and Israel's questioning their identity, including remembering the past and pondering the meaning of the exile.

In Book V, the figure of David points past his earthly kingship to the truth that "Israel's true monarch is . . . Yahweh" (McCann, 662). Familiar and trusted, the figure of David reminds exiles returning to rebuild their lives that God is their "protector, provider and sustainer" (deClaissé-Walford, 113). As in the past, their survival as a people hinges on honoring their covenant with God and on God's "steadfast love."

Deliverance from Chaos into Praise (Ps 107)

Prior to the doxology that ends Book IV, Psalm 106:47 pleads, "Save us, O LORD our God, and gather us from among the nations, that we may give thanks to your holy name and glory in your praise." Those scattered by defeat and exile pray for deliverance and reunion. Fragmented and distant, the people long to be gathered by God and to worship together again.

In Psalm 107:1-3, the speaker indicates that their plea has been answered (McCann, 1116): "O give thanks to the LORD, for he is good; for his steadfast love endures forever. Let the redeemed of the LORD say so, those he redeemed from trouble and gathered in from the lands, from the east and from the west and from the north and from the south."

God has ended the exile through King Cyrus of Persia and gathered the scattered Israelites back home. In response, as promised in 106:47, the people "give thanks" and praise to God.

The psalm offers four examples of people in distress: the "hungry and thirsty" in the desert, prisoners in "darkness and in gloom," those whose illnesses result from "sinful ways," and those in danger on the seas (vv. 5, 10, 17, 23). In each instance, those in distress cry out to God, God hears and delivers, and the people respond with praise and thanksgiving. Those in the desert are desperate for water, food, and shelter. They "cried out to the LORD in their trouble, and he delivered them from their distress," leading them to an "inhabited town" (v. 6). In response the speaker calls the people to "thank the LORD for his steadfast love . . . for he satisfies the thirsty, and the hungry he fills with good things" (vv. 8-9). This cycle of deliverance is familiar to Israel, etched into their story as God's people.

In the three following examples of distress, the people in danger "cried out to the LORD in their trouble," and he delivered them/saved them/brought them out from their distress (vv. 13, 19,

28). In each case, the speaker calls the people to "thank the LORD for his steadfast love" (vv. 15, 21, 31). Each situation receives a specific description of struggle and deliverance fitting its setting, but the refrains above tie all four together. In every situation of distress, the people cry out to God, God delivers them, and they receive a call to praise God in response.

Interestingly, there are two examples of deliverance from chaos and two of deliverance from sin (McCann, 1117). Chaos, represented by the desert and sea, is beyond human control. Only God can effect change in chaos, guiding the people to an "inhabited town" and making "the storms be still" (vv. 7, 29). When circumstances are far beyond our control, God brings salvation out of chaos (McCann, 1117).

Yet God also brings salvation when human sin has caused suffering. As we know well, human sin has consequences. Here we see loss of freedom by prisoners who "spurned the counsel of the Most High" and illness by those who were "sick through their sinful ways" (vv. 11, 17). Notably, the speaker does not link *all* illness to sin, but looks specifically to those whose illness was linked somehow to "affliction" (v. 17). For both the prisoners and the ill, God forgave, freeing the prisoners and healing the sick. Through forgiveness and salvation, God intervenes in the chaos humans create through our sin, as well as chaos beyond our influence.

The last ten verses of the psalm comprise a hymn of thanksgiving to God for justice and provision. Where the wicked abide, God turns good land into a "salty waste" (v. 34). But for the needy, God "turns a desert into pools of water . . . and there lets the hungry live and they establish a town" where they prosper through God's blessings (vv. 35-38). What good news for hungry and thirsty exiles who have come home anticipating God's continued blessings in their promised land.

At the same time, the people know to expect strife, as they have throughout their existence: "when they are diminished and brought low . . . he pours contempt on princes . . . but raises up the needy out of distress" (vv. 39-41). Once again, the psalmist names clearly the distress of being "diminished" just as the pain of the exile was voiced honestly throughout Book IV. Human pain and suffering are a given of living in a broken world.

But far more powerful is God's steadfast love in responding to the people's cries. They will not be in distress forever, and when deliverance comes, as it surely will, "wickedness stops its mouth" (v. 42). Love, justice, and blessing are God's final word.

Psalm 107 closes with a call to "give heed to these things and consider the steadfast love of the LORD" (v. 43). Pondering God's steadfast love is fitting instruction for a people newly returned to their decimated homeland. Everything has changed: Cyrus, though a more benevolent "prince" (v. 40) than Babylon's rulers, is earthly king over the Israelites. They have so much to do to rebuild their lives, homes, and temple. Yet God has "gathered them" back together as a people in the land of their ancestors. The exile may have changed them permanently, but God is still the One who hears their cries, delivers them, and provides for them. Thus, Psalm 107 calls the people to the only fitting response to such a deliverer: praise.

David Redux (Pss 108–110)

Psalm 107 calls the "redeemed" and "gathered" people to praise God (vv. 2-3), and Psalm 108 obliges with communal praises (vv. 1-5). Interestingly, Psalm 108 is made up of lines borrowed verbatim from Psalms 57:7-11 and 60:5-12. So though Psalm 108 begins with thanksgiving, the superscription from Psalm 57 indicates that the praises came when David was hiding in a cave from a murderous King Saul (1 Sam 22–24).

The call to "sing and make melody . . . awake, O harp and lyre . . . sing praises" to the Lord for God's "steadfast love" (57:7-10; 108:1-4) comes only after lament in Psalm 57. In serious danger, David cries out for deliverance from "those who trample on me" (57:3). The call to sing occurs only after deliverance has come, a response of praise to God after the enemies have fallen into a trap of their own making (57:6). Thus, while Psalm 108 begins with praise, in their original setting, these words arise in response to God's deliverance from a life-threatening situation.

In borrowing words of praise from a challenging time in David's life, the psalmist encourages the returned Israelites to celebrate and praise in the midst of their own uncertainty. Though times are hard, the people are now home, and God will be faithful to them, just as God was faithful to a "very human" King David throughout his life (deClaissé-Walford, 117). Like David, the people will "sing praises to you among the nations" (108:3), witnessing even as one of those nations rules over them.

Verses 6-13 come from Psalm 60:5-12, which includes a superscription referring to a national defeat linked to David's struggle with "Aram-naharaim and with Aram-zobah." In 2 Samuel 8:3-8 and 10:16-18, Israel ultimately defeated the Arameans, but there were likely defeats within the struggle. Psalm 60 asks God for "victory . . . so that those whom you love may be rescued" (60:3; 108:6). God responds by promising sanctuary, asserting power over areas of Israel and enemy territory by name (60:6-8; 108:7-9).

Knowing that "human help is worthless," the king pleads for God's help, asking, "Have you not rejected us, O God?" (60:10-11; 108:11-12). This is the same question the exiles have asked themselves. Retrofitting David's assurance to Israel's current situation, they declare in the final verse, "With God we shall do valiantly; it is he who will tread down our foes" (108:13). As with David, human help will not save the Israelites—only God can assure that they "do valiantly" and not only survive, but flourish.

Psalm 109 follows this community prayer for victory with an individual prayer of David for deliverance. David prays for vindication against those speaking falsely against him. He cries out for God's help: "Save me according to your steadfast love. Let them know that this is your hand. . . . Let them curse but you will bless" (vv. 26-28). In the setting of postexilic Israel, these words assure that nothing their enemies say against them will stand in the face of God's ultimate blessing. Regardless of human machinations, God's steadfast love will prevail.

Psalm 110 follows with a royal psalm, affirming the king as chosen and blessed by God. The words of affirmation offered to David transfer to the people who are now without an earthly king: "the LORD is at your right hand" (v. 5). Now, God is their only king. Cyrus may rule the Persian Empire, but the God of Israel rules all the nations.

The Egyptian *Hallel* Psalms (Pss 113–118)

Psalms 113–118 form a unit of *hallel* or praise psalms centered on Israel's deliverance from Egypt. In the Greek translation of the Old Testament known as the Septuagint, these psalms all have the superscription "Hallelujah! Praise the LORD!" Together they celebrate God's faithfulness in the past with exuberant praise. These psalms are traditionally read during Passover, the festival that commemorates the Israelites' exodus from captivity in Egypt (deClaissé-Walford, 118). By honoring God's steadfast love in history, the people also claim God's steadfast love in the present and for the future.

Psalms 113 and 114 begin the Passover celebration: "Praise the LORD! Praise, O servants of the LORD; praise the name of the LORD" (113:1); "From the rising of the sun to its setting the name of the LORD is to be praised" (113:3); "Who is like the LORD our God. . . . He raises the poor from the dust . . . to make them sit with princes" (113:5, 7, 8); "When Israel went out from Egypt . . . Judah became God's sanctuary, Israel his dominion. The sea looked and fled" (114:1-3); "Tremble, O earth, at the presence of the LORD" (114:7).

Psalms 115–118 end the celebration (deClaissé-Walford, 118): "Not to us, O LORD . . . but to your name give glory, for the sake of your steadfast love and your faithfulness" (115:1); "The LORD has been mindful of us; he will bless us" (115:12); "I love the LORD, because he has heard my voice and my supplications. . . . The snares of death encompassed me. . . . Then I called on the name of the LORD. . . . When I was brought low, he saved me" (116:1, 3, 4, 6); "Praise the LORD, all you nations! . . . The faithfulness of the LORD endures forever" (117:1, 2); "O give thanks to the LORD, for he is good. . . . It is better to take refuge in the LORD than to put confidence in princes. . . . The stone that the builders rejected has become the chief cornerstone. . . . This is the day that the LORD has made; let us rejoice and be glad in it. . . . O give thanks to the LORD, for he is good, his steadfast love endures forever" (118:1, 9, 22, 24, 29).

The reunited people of God have much for which to give thanks, especially deliverance from Babylon and return home. These psalms remind the people of all God has done through the years, using evocative language to call forth exuberant celebration. In uncertain times, remembering all God has done and celebrating past blessings help us reframe the present.

God's Law as Cornerstone (Ps 119)

The lengthiest psalm by far, Psalm 119 is an acrostic poem that exalts God's steadfast love and the wisdom of adhering to God's laws. Each of the twenty-two letters of the Hebrew alphabet begins an eight-line section. Within these 176 lines are hymns of thanksgiving, prayers for help, celebrations of God's Law, and encouragement to follow it. Fittingly, Psalm 119 is read at the Feast of Pentecost, which celebrates God's giving of the Torah (Law) to Moses at Mt. Sinai (deClaissé-Walford, 119).

Why would the people need to be reminded of God's Law as they rebuilt their lives as vassals under a foreign king? Why are they reminded "Happy are those . . . who walk in the law of the LORD?" (v. 1). Why are they called to be like the speaker who delights "in the way of your decrees" (v. 14)?

Rebuilding the temple and the holy city of Jerusalem and coming to terms with their new political reality were not easy tasks. Never again would Israel rule itself or know the prosperity it enjoyed under the house of David. The destruction of their God-given homeland and the temple where God chose to dwell, in addition to their exile to a foreign land, have been burned onto the people's collective memory. As they reestablish themselves in the land of their ancestors and create homes out of the rubble left to them, the people need to hear again, over and over, the goodness, wisdom, and necessity of following God's Law.

God gave the Law to bless the people, guiding them in right relationship with God and with one another, providing a "lamp to my feet and a light to my path" (v. 105). Israel's history proves that rejecting God's Law leads to troubled relationships with God and each other. Yet even when they keep divine law, trouble may still come: "I have become like a wineskin in the smoke, yet I have not forgotten your statutes" (v. 83). This unjust situation leads immediately to a plea for deliverance: "How long must your servant endure?. . . . Help me!" (vv. 84, 86), a cry echoed throughout Psalm 119.

Notably, the plea for deliverance comes so that the speaker may continue to meditate on God's laws (v. 97) as well as praise God's name (v. 171). The law is such a touchstone for the speaker's relationship with God that it tastes "sweeter than honey to my mouth!" (v. 103). The psalmist loves God's Law (v. 113), exclaiming, "The unfolding of your words gives light" (v. 130). Absent is any sense that God's Law is restrictive, but rather life-giving and fulfilling.

What good news for the returning exiles as they rebuild a life from destruction! In steadfast love, God has delivered them from Babylon and will deliver them from whatever trauma comes next. God's covenant love enables them to deeply engage with God's Law, living out daily covenant love with God and neighbor. The Law is God's cornerstone for their rebuilding together as God's people, just as it has been a cornerstone throughout their history. And that is a truth worthy of great praise.

As Christians, we hear in Psalm 119 roots of the good news of the gospel. Jesus came to fulfill the Law (Matt 5:17-20), and through his life, death, and resurrection, new life in God is made possible. All along, the Law pointed to an intimate, full, and nurturing relationship with God and one another. In Jesus, the Law is fulfilled in a way only God could fulfill: covenant love incarnate. Through Jesus' fulfillment of the Law, we are all invited to a deep, transformative relationship with God that is "sweeter than honey" (v. 103) and better than "thousands of gold and silver pieces" (v. 72).

Life Lessons

The first part of Book V draws deeply on Israel's past to inform and inspire its present. Recalling the days of David, a time of prosperity and security, reminds them that God is indeed at work and always has been, even when they could not see or understand. Focusing on past deliverance and offering praise center the people on God's steadfast love, the truest cornerstone throughout the ages. While rebuilding their lives in a radically changed Israel, the people needed constant reminders of that cornerstone in order to establish a solid foundation in the present and for their future.

Similarly, we call on these ancient hymns to deepen our faith and guide our steps. These psalms attest to the necessity of remembering the past as we navigate the present. Looking back, God's goodness takes clearer form. We can see how God was working in hindsight and how deliverance was on the way even when we couldn't see it. Those memories secure us in God's steadfast love as we struggle to live faithfully in the present. They remind us of the cornerstone on which our lives depend.

We live in a what-have-you-done-for-me-lately world that runs at the speed of anxiety. But we were created for relationship and crafted for remembering. In remembering, we recall who and whose we are, which enables us to live securely in the present—and into a future that belongs to God.

1. When have you felt the type of chaos described in 107:4-32? Describe what it was like to live in that chaos.

2. How did God deliver you from the worst of the chaos? What was it like to see it end? How have you praised God for that deliverance?

3. Revisiting Psalm 108, have you ever borrowed from past experience (your own or someone else's) to help yourself in the present? When has past hardship and deliverance informed a present crisis in your life?

4. The *hallel* psalms (113–118) celebrate liberation from Egypt, which happened millennia before the return of the exiles. Do you see modern believers praising God for long-past blessings? How might doing so inform the present?

5. What might our tendency to minimize or forget past blessings say about us? How is this like Israel's tendency to forget God and God's constancy in remembering Israel?

6. Does Psalm 119's emphasis on God's Law appeal to you or not? How is the Law framed as a blessing rather than a limitation? How might your perception of Psalm 119 change if we substituted "teaching" for "Law"?

7. In the spirit of these psalms that remember, think back to past experiences of God's deliverance and blessing. List some of those experiences here. Offer God a prayer of praise and thanksgiving for all God has done in your life.

8. How does offering praise to God for past blessings inform your approach to present struggles? What is it like to first offer praise for past blessings, remembering all God has done, and then ask for help with present concerns?

9. Consider offering praise for God's gifts of deliverance each day for a week, possibly using Psalm 113 or 117 as a touchstone. Note how your outlook on current issues changes over the week.

_____
_____
_____
_____
_____

Session 9

Moving With and Toward God

Book V: Psalms 120–122, 127, 130

I suspect that the notion of *pilgrimage* is foreign to many of us. The idea of traveling to a specific holy site in order to worship God in that place is not high on our list of religious priorities, perhaps due to an emphasis on God's presence everywhere. Any place can be a holy place if we give our attention to the Lord while we're in that place.

Ancient Israelites believed in God's ubiquitous presence (Ps 139) but also attached huge significance to the city of Jerusalem. Jews, Christians, and Muslims of our own day consider the city holy, which is why the "holy city" remains a hotly contested city. Then and now, a pilgrimage to Jerusalem for many people was/is one of life's greatest desires.

Not surprisingly, *pilgrim psalms* developed in Israel to be sung as travelers were making their way to Jerusalem. As Book V of the psalter explores the contours of life after exile, when many Israelites had come home, it is no surprise that a collection of pilgrim psalms would be given a prominent place in the book. Each psalm from Psalm 120 through 134 is called in its superscription "A Song of Ascents." Since Jerusalem was set on a mountain, pilgrims had to travel "up" to the city. They would sing these songs all along the way as they made the ascent to their spiritual home.

It's Time to Move (Ps 120)

Psalm 120 makes no mention of Jerusalem, but instead focuses on what motivates people to go on pilgrimage. Pilgrimage to Jerusalem is commanded, to be sure (Deut 16:16), but often much more is at stake. Distress, characterized here by enemies who lie and slander, creates a hostile environment from which the pilgrim longs to escape: "Too long have I had my dwelling among those who hate peace. I am for peace; but when I speak, they are for war" (vv. 6-7). No author is named in the superscription, nor is the author's location verified. Whoever he or she is, the current context is not safe, and the hope of a better place gets the psalmist on the move.

As the first psalm of ascent, Psalm 120 is "a poignant expression of pilgrims' pain over the world from which they come. It puts that world in sharpest contrast to the peace they desire and seek in coming to Zion" (Mays, 385). Those who set out on the way are seeking a peace not found in their actual homes—a peace with God and with neighbor that they hope to experience in their spiritual home, Jerusalem.

The beginning of the Jerusalem pilgrimage works nicely as a metaphor for the Christian journey, as a person "has to be thoroughly disgusted with the way things are to find the motivation to set out on the Christian way . . . before he, before she, acquires an appetite for the world of grace" (Peterson, *A Long Obedience*, 21). Recently, I met with a man who reached a place of disgust and desperation because of a battle with alcohol and drugs. He'd had enough, and he wanted to change, so he cried out to God in prayer, started coming to church, and started attending Alcoholics Anonymous meetings. He has a long way to go, but he has acquired an appetite for the world of grace and embarked on a pilgrimage with Jesus.

On the Move (Ps 121)

Psalm 120 establishes that it's time to move, and Psalm 121 gets us out on the road. The psalmist does not travel alone to Jerusalem, nor does the psalmist have to arrive at the destination before experiencing God's presence. The Lord is present every step of the way, actively watching over the psalmist and evoking the confession, "My help comes from the LORD, who made heaven and earth" (121:2).

Six times, the psalm affirms in some fashion that God will "keep" the pilgrim. God will not let go, will not lose, and will not discard, but will always protect and provide for the psalmist. The constancy of the Lord's "keeping" is portrayed in the truth that "he who keeps you will not slumber. He who keeps Israel will neither slumber nor sleep" (vv. 3-4). There is attention to the individual and to Israel as a whole, as the Lord "keeps" unceasingly the individual pilgrim along with the entire community. The pilgrim and the people may grow tired and weary, but the One who keeps them does not know fatigue and thus is able to provide constant help and attention.

I don't know how or when I developed this pastoral practice, but for at least twenty years now I've concluded every prayer at a hospital bedside asking God to hold the individual "in your care, and hold us all in your care." It's an expression of our belief that "no place, no time, no circumstance will be able to separate the psalmist from God's loving care" (McCann, 1181). Paul puts it this way in Romans 8:39, saying that nothing "will be able to separate us from the love of God in Christ Jesus our Lord." Psalm 121 shares a similar perspective: "The LORD will keep your going out and your coming in from this time on and forevermore" (v. 8). Whether the journey is to Jerusalem or some other destination, or our life's journey with God and neighbor, it is always undertaken in the presence and care of God.

Arriving at Our Destination (Ps 122)

Psalm 120 says it's time to move, Psalm 121 gets us on the move, and by Psalm 122 we arrive at the destination. Perhaps you've prayed verse 1 on Sunday mornings before church or at church: "I was glad when they said to me, 'Let us go to the house of the LORD!'" It's the perfect prayer to pray wherever we happen to be on Sunday mornings, but in its original context it was an expression of sheer joy at being in Jerusalem and about to enter the temple. The journey is over, the pilgrims have arrived in the holy city, and now they can say, "Our feet are standing within your gates, O Jerusalem" (v. 2).

As with all the psalms, it is hard to date the exact time of composition for Psalm 122. It seems to reflect a time when Solomon's temple was standing and kings from the line of David were still in power, as it states that in Jerusalem "the thrones of judgment were set up, the thrones of the house of David" (v. 5). Its context within Book V of the psalter, however, suggests that this psalm continued to be sung after the original temple had been destroyed and a second, less glorious temple had been built.

Whether in the time of David and his heirs or in the time after the exile when many Israelites had come home or could travel home on pilgrimage, the peace of Jerusalem was always a concern. Foreign armies constantly attacked Davidic kings and their armies, and in the time after the exile, Israel lived under the thumb of one foreign power after another. So those who sing this song while standing in Jerusalem's gates say to themselves and their fellow Israelites everywhere, "Pray for the peace of Jerusalem: 'May they prosper who love you. Peace be within your walls and security within your towers. . . . For the sake of the house of God, I will seek your good" (vv. 6-7, 9).

The need to pray for Jerusalem's peace remains today, yet the bewildering political context of competing claims by citizens of the modern state of Israel and their Palestinian neighbors can make it hard to know how to pray. It's helpful to note that the motivation to travel that we find in Psalm 120 and the hope to find peace in Jerusalem are not ultimately rooted in a place, but in God. Peace is not primarily a characteristic of a "holy city," but of a holy God, which means that "to enter Jerusalem is ultimately to experience the reality of God's reign and to be transformed to represent God's just purposes in God's world" (McCann, 1185).

Having become ambassadors of God's reign through our faith in Jesus, we pray not for a solution where there are winners and losers, but for a vision of peace and reconciliation. A dear friend is working hard for Jerusalem's peace by bringing together Israeli Christians, Palestinian Christians, and American Christians, inspired by the conviction that if those who are one in Christ can overcome their differences and embody the peace of Christ, then the dream of a larger peace will be furthered. In addition to praying for leaders, soldiers, and civilians, we pray for the peace of Jerusalem when we pray for people like my friend and his work and for the church in Jerusalem, Palestine, and the Middle East.

Work and Family: In God's Strength and for God's Purposes (Ps 127)

The pilgrimage to Jerusalem functioned for Israel and for followers of Jesus as a metaphor for the journey of life. Then and now, the temptation to undertake this journey in our own strength was and is very strong. It seems we human beings are forever trying to earn our way, prove ourselves, establish our worth, and control our own destinies.

Whether the pilgrimage of life is set in postexilic Israel or in twenty-first-century America, Psalm 127 keeps us anchored in the truth that our work is dependent on God's work. More accurately, it is God who works through our efforts to get the job done: "Unless the LORD builds the house, those who build it labor in vain. Unless the LORD guards the city, the guard keeps watch in vain" (vv. 1-2).

We are full participants as we learn our craft, develop our skills, and discipline ourselves to stay on task until the work is completed. But all our "efforts will come to no good end unless they are undertaken as part of God's purposes in the world" (Brueggemann and Bellinger, 543). Whatever our work, we're called to make sure it's in line with God's reign. We're called to work with an awareness of God working through us and to depend on God in all we do.

When our work does not align with God's purposes and when we seek to keep ourselves at the center of it, the results are not good: "It is in vain that you rise up early and go late to rest, eating the bread of anxious toil" (v. 2). In addition to naming Psalm 127 "A Song of Ascent," the superscription also says it is "Of Solomon." Solomon is the poster child of excess in Israelite history, from the size of his palace to the number of his wives, yet Ecclesiastes 1:2 tells his story when it says, "Vanity of vanities, all is vanity." In other words, all the things human effort can accomplish on their own are like a breath, a vapor, both in how long they last and the impact they have. But when we embrace work as the privilege of partnering with God in the world and not as the means by which we make our own way, and when we trust God as we work instead of being consumed with worry over whether or not all will go well with our work, we discover that "he gives sleep to his beloved" (v. 2). Sleep comes from the satisfaction that we have done our part, but more importantly from the awareness that our work and its results are in God's hands. Work and sleep are both gifts from the One on whom we depend.

Family life is the focus of the second half of the psalm, especially the gift of sons: "Sons are indeed a heritage from the LORD" (v. 3). Verses 3-5 reflect the Wisdom traditions of ancient Israel and other ancient societies organized around a patriarchal system. Ownership of property passed from father to son, not father or mother to daughter. Leadership in society was usually reserved for men. Economic transactions occurred in an arena dominated by men. Many sons gave a father many partners with whom to participate and advance in a society economically and politically dominated by men. Such a father "shall not be put to shame when he speaks with his enemies at the gate" (v. 5) because he will not face his enemies alone. The presence of many sons gives the father an economic, political, and physical edge over his enemies.

We no longer live in a completely patriarchal society, and New Testament passages like Galatians 3:28 ("there is no longer male and female; for all of you are one in Christ Jesus") tell us that Jesus sets us free from patriarchy in all its forms. So how do we apply to our day a psalm that ignores daughters and mothers and focuses completely on fathers and sons? By exploring the intersection of work (vv. 1-2) and family (vv. 3-5).

The city gate in ancient times was the arena where serious economic transactions took place and legal disputes were settled (v. 5). A father with many sons had many advantages in this arena. Today, a person with many children gains no competitive advantage in the marketplace and might be at a competitive disadvantage because of the amount of resources those children tie up. Unlike agricultural societies, where many children are necessary as workers in order for the family to survive, children in today's economically successful families produce nothing and consume massive amounts of the family's income. The family pours financial and emotional resources into its children for eighteen to twenty-two years (or more) to help them arrive at a time when they can "make it on their own."

Instead of viewing the family as an economic or emotional unit, Psalm 127 as a whole invites us to view families as "mission teams" called to do God's work wherever they are, utilizing the gifts that God has given to each member of the family. Combining the focus on faithful work (vv. 1-2) with the awareness that children increase the ability of their parents to do the work God has called them to do (vv. 3-5), we realize that a family's primary purpose "is not to achieve economic prosperity or even happiness, but to love and serve God and meet the needs of other people" (Campolo and Campolo, 180). Such a family looks for ways it can minister together, from visiting nursing homes (little children are often a far greater blessing than their parents in visiting the elderly!) to going on mission trips together to making financial decisions together based on how they can best give to their church and to other organizations that do God's kingdom work.

Knowing that "no projects are completed unless they are embedded in the larger purposes of God" (Mays, 127), such families will not strive to build the house (that is, do the work of God) on their own, but will trust in the Lord to work through them. They will offer their service in God's strength and trust the results to the Lord. At the gate, in the church, and around the neighborhood, parents and children who trust and serve the Lord together will not be put to shame, but will be the light of Christ in their community.

Out of the Depths (Ps 130)

We don't know what the depths are when the psalmist cries, "Out of the depths I cry to you, O LORD" (130:1). Perhaps it's the depths of illness or emotional depression or physical danger. We are familiar with the depths. When a difficult diagnosis is received, when a job is lost, when a dream comes to an end, or when a loved one dies, we often enter a personal depth from which it feels like there's no way out. On the journey to Jerusalem, pilgrims had this psalm to remind them that the journey of life is not always an *ascent*, but often a *descent* into the depths.

Yet it's often in the depths that we become more aware of our need for God than in any other place. No effort is made here to climb out of the depths, and no plans are devised to make escape possible because the only real option is to yell, "LORD, hear my voice! Let your ears be attentive to the voice of my supplications!" (v. 2). Whatever the situation is, the psalmist quickly assesses it and knows that only the Lord can make a way out of it. I suspect that many of us, myself included, are not quite as quick to cry out to the Lord. Often, we try to climb out of the depths on our own. When that fails, we try to endure and make do in the depths, but that's not sustainable either. We tend to exhaust all other options before crying out in desperation like the psalmist. Yet all indications are that crying out to the Lord is not only the *first* option but the *only* option for this faithful Israelite caught in the depths.

We've seen the demanding tone of verse 2 often in our journey through Psalms. The assumptions behind the verse are breathtaking for those of us raised to be "nice" in prayer. The psalmist dares to assume that God is not attentive at the current moment and dares to believe that by demanding to be heard, God will snap to attention in response.

But the demanding tone doesn't last long. A confession of sin and praise for God's forgiveness follow in verses 3-4: "If you, O LORD, should mark iniquities, LORD, who could stand? But there is forgiveness with you, so that you may be revered." God does not walk around with a heavenly score card, marking this sin and that sin until enough marks accumulate to warrant a specific punishment. If that were the case, then no chalkboard could have enough space to contain every mark necessary to record your sins and mine, and none of us could stand under the weight. Instead, God's nature is to forgive our sins and restore our lives.

Note that the reason for forgiveness is not so punishment can be avoided and guilt absolved. Instead of the removal of a negative consequence, forgiveness here focuses on the bestowal of a positive action. We are forgiven so we can revere God. Forgiveness "gets us back in the game" so to speak, restoring us to our proper role of loving God and neighbor.

Often, people confess their sins and believe in their minds they are forgiven, but in their hearts they're not so sure. After the confession is made and forgiveness is received, they remain shy about approaching God. The sense may be that they need to work their way back into God's good graces before they can really pray and love. Certainly the consequences to our relationships are not done away with when God forgives us, and repentance does involve seeking to right the wrongs we've done. But verse 4 suggests that a waiting period is not required before our relationship with God is renewed. We are forgiven for the specific purpose of getting us back to the place where we revere, honor, and praise God.

As we arrive at verse 5, there is no indication that the psalmist has been rescued from the depths, but the mood has been transformed: "I wait for the LORD, my soul waits, and in his word I hope." This waiting "is not impatiently watching the time pass. It is rather anticipating that divine forgiveness and a new beginning will come" (Brueggemann and Bellinger, 551). God has heard, God is now attentive, and soon God will act.

A non-anxious eagerness and a confident assurance now allows the psalmist to say, "My soul waits for the LORD more than those who watch for the morning, more than those who watch for the morning" (v. 6). Those who watch for the morning could be the guards who watch over the city through the night and wait for the sun to appear, signaling that they've made it safely through the dark hours. Or this could be an allusion "to the fact that confirmation of God's help often came in the early morning after a night of praying and waiting" (Miller, 922). Either way, the eyes of the psalmist's soul are wide open, watching and waiting for an ascent from the depths by the mercies of God.

A shift occurs in verse 7. To this point the focus has been on one individual down in the depths, but now all of Israel is addressed. Book V speaks to Israel's continuing existence under the thumb of foreign powers, which means that even though it is now possible for the Jerusalem pilgrimage to be made, the nation in many ways is very much in the depths. To the people as a whole the psalmist says,

"O Israel, hope in the LORD! For with the LORD there is steadfast love, and with him is great power to redeem" (vv. 7-8). The sins of a *person* in verse 3 are now joined to the sins of a *people* in verse 7. Both are equally serious, and both can be forgiven, not because of the importance of the sinners, but because of the power of God. As they make their way toward Jerusalem, pilgrims are given language to voice their individual confession of sin and to confess sin on behalf of their fellow Israelites, all the while knowing "it is he who will redeem Israel from all its iniquities" (v. 8).

Life Lessons

The psalms of ascent sung by pilgrims on the way to Jerusalem invite us to think of our lives as journeys with God and each other. The Jerusalem pilgrimage could be divided into various stages, from starting out to moving forward to arriving at the destination, as reflected in Psalms 120–122. Chronologically, at what stage of the journey do you find yourself right now? In our younger years we may have more physical energy for the journey, in our older years we may have more wisdom for the journey, but at all stages of life's journey we're called to do our part in God's ongoing work in the world.

A crucial element in thinking of our life as a journey is being fully present to the current stage of the journey. Though the past shapes who we are and invites intentional reflection so we can understand ourselves better, and though the future deserves our best planning and dreaming, the present moment demands our best attention. In this sense, to "wait for the LORD" (130:5) is to do more than anticipate God's future actions. It is to place our future in God's hands so we can love God and neighbor right now. To know that the Lord is our "keeper" (121:5) is to be set free to embrace the present stage of the journey since our lives are always in the hands of the One who keeps our going out and our coming in.

1. Discuss the quotation from Eugene Peterson that a person "has to be thoroughly disgusted with the way things are to find the motivation to set out on the Christian way . . . before he, before she, acquires an appetite for the world of grace." Does this ring true in your experience?

2. What does it mean for the Lord to "keep" you and to "keep your going out and your coming in" (121:8)?

3. In a culture where worship attendance is declining, how do we help people embrace the words "I was glad when they said to me, 'Let us go to the house of the Lord!'" (122:1)?

4. How do you pray for peace in Jerusalem and in other parts of the world?

5. What is the difference between hard work done with trust in God and anxious toil?

6. What are ways that families of all ages can be "mission teams"? How can churches equip and empower families for their missions?

7. How does the idea that God forgives sin so that we can revere God (130:4) fit into your overall understanding of forgiveness?

8. What is the next step of spiritual growth that God is leading you to in this stage of your journey? What are the next steps of service to which God is calling you in this stage?

Session 10

Prayers for a Full Life
Psalms 135–150

Following the songs of ascent, the last part of Book V continues the themes of praise and lament so richly embroidered throughout Psalms. David ponders the vastness of God and pleads for deliverance from trouble. The wonder of creation and the events of the exodus occupy the psalmists, as do God's attention to Jerusalem and care for Israel. Notably, the final five psalms close the book with hymns of praise, ending Israel's authentic, revealing conversation with God with a decisive call to praise the Giver of all good things.

Praising the Covenant-er, Creator, and Liberator (Pss 135–136)

"Praise the LORD!" provides bookends for Psalm 135, a community hymn of praise. Between the bookends, the psalmist weaves together allusions to numerous biblical texts, creating a multifaceted, scripturally rich song of praise. By including echoes of so many passages familiar to ancient Israel, the speaker shapes the people's worship through memory.

The initial call to praise springs forth because God "is gracious," having chosen "Israel as his own possession" (vv. 3-4), a reference to the covenant language of Exodus 19:5 and Deuteronomy 7:6. Both passages from the Torah clarify that God has chosen Israel out of divine steadfast love, not because of "the nation's intrinsic value" (McBride, 280). The clear focus of this hymn is God's goodness, orienting all who pray this psalm toward God, fully immersing them in worship.

The speaker continues offering reasons to praise God by borrowing from other scriptural images for God as Creator and Lord over all (vv. 5-7). Then comes praise for God's liberation of the people from Egypt and defeat of kings who threatened them on their way home to the promised land (vv. 8-12; some of these conflicts are described in Num 21:21-35; Deut 2:26–3:11). As in other psalms, key events of the exodus, the wilderness struggles, and settling of Canaan remind the people why God deserves praise.

The psalmist also contrasts the living God of Israel with idols from other nations (vv. 15-18). These idols, "the work of human hands," cannot respond to human cries for help like the God of Israel (v. 15). The covenant-God liberates the people from Egypt and settles them in a homeland. The idols are silent and foolish in comparison.

With all these reasons to praise, how can the "house of Israel" not "bless the LORD?" (v. 19) The priestly houses of Aaron and Levi and even "you that fear the LORD," a possible reference to non-Israelites who have joined the people, are called to join the praise. A final "hallelujah!" or "praise the LORD" closes this exuberant, joyful call to praise.

Psalm 136 continues this call to praise, expanding on God's saving acts of steadfast love throughout Israel's history. This hymn is arranged as a litany, with the leader offering praise for God's goodness and the people responding "for his steadfast love endures forever" each time. The leader first extols the goodness and sovereignty of God (vv. 1-3) before turning to the wonders of creation (vv. 4-9) and the details of the exodus, wilderness days, and the settling of the land. A summary then praises God for remembering and rescuing the people, as well as providing for "all flesh," ending with a final "for his steadfast love endures forever" (vv. 23-26).

The litany form invites worshipers to join fully in the praise, voicing together the reminder we constantly need: God's steadfast love endures forever. Throughout Psalms, human frailty and fault come through clearly and authentically. But God's goodness is the touchstone, the tie that binds the people together with their covenant-God. Giving thanks is the only fitting response to God's steadfast love and faithfulness—a reminder we all need regularly in a world that views worship as a "royal 'waste' of time" (Dawn).

Grief, Remembrance, and an Angry Cry for Justice (Ps 137)

Psalm 137 is one of the most disturbing imprecatory psalms because of its vividly violent final verse: "Happy shall they be who take your little ones and dash them against the rock!" Most modern uses of this psalm in worship remove this final verse. Our hearts and minds simply cannot fathom such a horrible reaction to anyone—even an "enemy."

Yet we remember that Israel's tradition encouraged and even expected honest, intimate, no-holds-barred interaction with God. The intimacy of the covenant invited unguarded speech. Unlike our modern, cleaned-up prayers, the psalmists offered even their most impulsive outbursts to God, the only place where transformation of even our deepest sin is possible.

Scholar Eric Zenger proposes an alternate title for Psalm 137 to reframe how we hear the text: "What Remains for the Powerless" (Zenger, 47). By framing the entire psalm, including the vividly disturbing final verse, as a cry for an end to suffering, we can better understand the context and layers of meaning of the passage. Voiced from the valley of the shadow, the psalm's poetic, evocative first portion unfolds into a call for justice from a people who have been decimated.

Psalm 137 is clearly a lament, a deep communal outpouring of grief about the demoralizing events of the exile to Babylon. As we remember, the Babylonians, the superpower and unstoppable "war machine" (Zenger, 50) of the region, decimated Jerusalem and destroyed the temple. This defeat would change Israel forever, in line with the importance of the exodus and the giving of the Ten Commandments. But this time, God did not deliver the people from their troubles. The trouble just kept coming. The Babylonians did not simply want to defeat the people and rule them. They wanted to *destroy the identity and religion of the Israelites completely*. The goal of this superpower was to erase Israel from the earth.

The Babylonians rounded up the temple leaders, the educated and educators, the sages and pillars of Israel and marched them to Babylon. The intention was to remove anyone who might help the Israelites recover from this defeat. The larger goal was to force the exiled Israelites to become like the Babylonians, melding into the larger population, thus losing their identity as God's "treasured possession" (Deut 7:6).

As modern readers, we might enter the context of Psalm 137 by comparing the exile to the Nazi Holocaust in its effects on the people (McCann, 1229). Though the Babylonians did not try to exterminate all Jews, the goal of ending the people of Israel was the same. Many Israelites died during the destruction of Jerusalem. Survivors were stripped of power and possessions, homes and support systems. Rounded up and carted away, families were divided, places of worship defiled, the God of Israel mocked, and the Israelites' identity as God's people ridiculed. All of this sounds painfully familiar to any who lived through or have studied the events of the Holocaust in the 1930s and 1940s.

When we place the words of Psalm 137 in the mouths of sufferers—ripped from their homes, powerless, mocked, and oppressed—the verses sound different. The speakers are not middle-class Americans, unaware of their privilege or power; they are the downtrodden, the demoralized, the shamed and beaten. They weep for their memories of home (v. 1) and cannot possibly sing the worship hymns of praise that once defined them (v. 2).

Their captors mock them openly, tormenting the already wounded by asking them to sing "one of the songs of Zion!" (v. 3). The scoffing reveals the Babylonians' belief that Israel's God was overpowered by Babylonian gods and has abandoned the Israelites. Sing praise to your defeated God, the Babylonians provoke. But "all the music has been knocked out of" the Israelites (Peterson, *Answering God*, 96).

But the people know already that they could not "sing the LORD's song in a foreign land" (v. 4). Silently, they remember Jerusalem and home, where God's presence was felt and real and powerful (vv. 5-6). No words, no songs can capture their grief fully. They vow together never to forget what they have lost, resisting the Babylonians' attempts to erase them through defeat, demoralization, and displacement.

Powerless and traumatized, they ask God to remember the complicity of the Edomites who had "joined in the sacking and pillaging of Jerusalem and handed over the fleeing survivors to the Babylonians" as found in Obadiah 8–14 and Ezekiel 25:12-14 and 35:2-9 (Miller, 927). Again, we can compare the Edomites' actions to the role of many non-Jews in Nazi territories who turned against their Jewish neighbors by reporting on them, hunting them, and turning them over to what often became sure death. Even neighbors turned against the Israelites; there was no quarter anywhere.

The anguish of the Israelites pours out to God and against their oppressors: "O Babylon, you devastator! Happy shall they be who pay you back for what you have done to us!" (v. 8). The oppressed want the oppressors to feel the pain they have inflicted, to learn what it means to lose all that Israel has lost. The traumatized want the perpetrators—who are so sure they will always be on top—to taste the devastation they doled out so ruthlessly. The grief of loss and trauma often includes "anger and outrage" (McCann, 1228); ignoring that part of grief only limits our healing.

The defeated, wounded Israelites want the Babylonian war machine to end, to stop its violent conquest of anyone and everyone in its way. They want "restoration of the world order" and call upon the only power that might be able to "put Babylon in its place" (Zenger, 50). Notably, they are not asking for a reversal of power so that they dominate the Babylonians, but that the Babylonian "reign of terror" should end (Zenger, 50). In the imagery of the psalm, Israel has been the helpless child smashed against the rocks (Zenger, 50), a reflection of the violence of warfare of the day (McCann, 1228). In desperation, the Israelites call for the same to be done to Babylon.

But this is not just about revenge—it is the cry to stop the next generation of Babylonians from continuing the empire's violent, dominating outlook on the world. War machines require young, indoctrinated soldiers to fill the ranks. Israel wants Babylon's long cycle of violence *to end with this generation* (Zenger, 50). In this snapshot of grief and anger, ending the next generation is the only way they can imagine stopping Babylon's reign of terror.

Though horrifyingly vivid, verse 9 is not a literal call for the extermination of all Babylonian children. This is not a "plan of action" (Zenger, 50), like Pharaoh's orders to throw all Hebrew baby boys into the Nile (Exod 1:22). Rather, it is a desperate cry that Babylon's "royal . . . dynasty of terror . . . be exterminated completely" (Zenger, 50). The "context of war" is the setting (Brueggemann and Bellinger, 576), and Israel cries out for the trauma to end.

Imagine this desperate cry for the end of terror's reign in the mouths of concentration camp prisoners. Those suffering at the hands of an unthinkably cruel regime may survive by imagining the day when that regime ends, tasting some of the pain they have caused. We can only imagine the anguished grief—including anger, rage, a cry for vengeance, and the end to such terror—that Holocaust survivors experienced.

While human vengeance is at play in verse 9, it is voiced in the only setting where it may be transformed: prayer. In sharing their anger and desperation with God, using the most vivid language they could muster, the people of God capture the frank reality of where they are at that moment. As much as we resist verse 9, "our hate needs to be prayed," offered to God when it wells up against evil that violates "the holiness of being" (Peterson, *Answering God*, 98). Honestly faced, hate becomes our "emotional link with the spirituality of evil" (Peterson, *Answering God*, 98), demanding that we face the evil we see, name it, and pray for its end.

At the same time, praying our hate also allows us to tell the truth about ourselves. Hate is "the ugliest and most dangerous of our emotions, the hair trigger on a loaded gun" (Peterson, *Answering God*, 98). Left untold and unexamined, hate may take deep root and wreak havoc in us and in our relationships.

So the Israelites place the snapshot of their hate into God's hands, where it will not remain as it is. Instead of pretending things are otherwise, the Israelites look evil in the eye, find it rampant, and refuse to turn away. They grapple with it in prayer, "channeling it in effective ways, in covenantal shapes" (Peterson, *Answering God*, 99).

Today's believers might tend to excise the truth about our darkest feelings, hiding our anguish, hate, or grief. We may try to jump to forgiveness before we've even processed the horror of a serious wrong done to us. We may try to mask the power of our "negative" emotions, which can markedly slow the healing process.

But the Israelites, a "tougher breed" spiritually (Peterson, *Answering God*, 98), take a completely different approach, as they have throughout Psalms. The Israelites refuse to minimize the evil they have experienced, and in telling the truth they entrust that truth to God, who will somehow redeem and transform the experience. The grief, anger, and hate they feel in response to evil will not deform them with bitterness in the end because they have captured it in prayer and will do so repeatedly. They have turned the last word over to God, who will make sure that verse 9 is not the last word.

As modern readers, we still may feel uncomfortable with verse 9. And we should—the imagery *should* shock us! May we let it shock us into looking more closely at the suffering in our world, looking evil in the eye instead of turning away and back to the comforts we enjoy. If we let it, Psalm 137 invites us to tell the truth about the deepest anguish of our world and our own lives—and handing those truths over and over again to God in prayer.

If we are looking for authentic transformation, then cutting out the embarrassing truths about ourselves, our histories, and our collective stories will not do. If we long for deeper communion with

God and each other, the truth is a good place to start—even, and especially, if it isn't pretty.

The Inescapable God (Ps 139)

Psalm 139 offers deeply comforting assurances of God's intimate knowledge of and presence with us. The psalm holds together God's role as sovereign, all-knowing Creator and personally invested Presence. The human is "enclosed in divine reality" with "awareness of the Lord as the total environment of life" (Mays, 425).

The speaker begins with God's intimate knowledge of him in the first six verses. Nothing he does, says, or even thinks escapes God's awareness. The psalmist celebrates God's close attention with awe: "Such knowledge . . . too wonderful for" him (v. 6).

The speaker turns to God's presence, from which he cannot "flee" even if he wanted to do so (v. 7). Even in Sheol, Israel's place of the dead usually noted for its absence of the divine, God is there (v. 8). Not even darkness can hide the speaker from God, to whom "the night is as bright as the day" (v. 11). *Darkness* conveys not just absence of light, but also spiritual difficulty: God sees through the darkness of any struggle and is able to understand it and see its end when we cannot.

God's presence at the speaker's creation occupies verses 13-18. God is the weaver who crafted the human form in his mother's womb, "in secret" as in the "depths of the earth," hidden from human understanding (vv. 13, 15). At the very beginning, God was intimately involved in the life of the speaker, forming a future for him (v. 16). Again, the speaker's response is awe: "How weighty are your thoughts, O God! How vast is the sum of them!" (v. 17).

Then a sudden turn occurs as the psalmist focuses on the wicked and prays for their destruction (vv. 19-24) so that God's will can be done (McCann, 1237). This imprecation specifically names "the bloodthirsty . . . who lift themselves up against you for evil!" (vv. 19-20). The speaker claims these enemies of God as his own enemies, hating them with "a perfect hatred," conveying a complete rejection of those who reject and are hostile to God (Brueggemann and Bellinger, 584). The speaker wants to be absolutely clear that he holds no truck with any who mock God and harm others.

The closing verses invite further searching and even testing (vv. 23-24). The speaker is willing to be judged by God, tested and examined for his own "wicked" ways. Secure in a trusting, dependent relationship with the God who knows him better than he knows himself, the psalmist longs for all wickedness—including his own—to be destroyed.

As with Psalm 137, the psalmist voices imprecations *in prayer*, leaving the situation with God the Creator, who alone can judge the creatures in the end. The psalmist knows the effects of the bloodthirsty and desperately wants justice to stop their rampage against God and humanity. Yet he also wants to root out any wickedness in himself—something only God can help him do through prayer: "A person's relationship to evil and injustice then becomes a matter of honest searching before the one divine judge in the context of the faith community" (Brueggemann and Bellinger, 584).

As usual with imprecatory passages, our Christian sensibilities may be disturbed. Hate? Loathe? Kill? That is not what Jesus taught us! Yet we are invited to hear the imprecation as a rejection of evil, which is as real in our lives as it was in that of the Israelites'. If we are complacent with human trafficking, exploitation, child pornography, or abuse, these imprecations jerk us out of our reveries to face the trauma of real life from the underside. While many modern believers seek to live out "hate the sin, love the sinner," these imprecatory parts of the psalms remind us that evil, in ourselves and all around us, is something indeed to reject and pray against. As we reject the evil we encounter and pray for its end, we place that evil and our response to it in the hands of the true judge, where it belongs.

Ending on a Praise Note (Pss 146–150)

We might describe believers today as having a "praise deficiency." Compared to the Israelites, our capacity for unadulterated, unrestrained sheer joy in worship appears to be anemic much of the time. Overwhelmed by the pace and demand of modern life, it is easy for us to forget that the sacrifice God asks for is thanksgiving (50:14), as well as a contrite heart (51:17).

The final five psalms overflow with praise and thanksgiving. Poetically beautiful, these verses call us to thank God for creation, as well as mercy, love, providence, nurture, justice, deliverance, healing, wisdom, and care for the oppressed. Reading all five psalms in a row underscores our role as God's creatures, fully dependent, fully loved, and fully responsive to God's goodness.

In the face of all this goodness, praise erupts from God's people. Singing and dancing and playing instruments enliven the offering of thanksgiving. All God's people join together because the "whole duty of humans is to praise and enjoy God" (Brueggemann and Bellinger, 619).

Life Lessons

The last five psalms invite us to ponder the role of praise in our lives. Do we see praise as our duty or "chief end," as the Westminster Shorter Catechism puts it? How often do we praise God with abandon? What would it look like if we intentionally made praise a more integral part of our spiritual life?

The psalmists knew their enemies, both physical and spiritual, were powerful. They struggled against all that opposes God. And they also knew exactly where to place that struggle: in the hands of God. Further, they knew that along with their struggles came bountiful blessings. The interweaving of lament and praise throughout the psalter calls us to consider the authenticity of our own prayer lives as a people and as individuals. Fully and openly, Israel wept and raged; fully and openly, Israel praised and celebrated God.

The book of Psalms is indeed the church's prayer book. If we tell the truth about ourselves, then these are our prayers, all 150 messy, embarrassing, shocking, honest, bone-deep offerings. If we are looking for ten easy steps to prayer, then the psalms are not the right option. But if we want to deepen our relationships with God and each other, our understanding of ourselves and of Scripture, and open ourselves up for transformation, then the psalms are exactly the right word.

1. Psalms 135–136 again use memory as a vital part of praise and use both remembering and praise as key elements of worship. How do your faith memories inform your practices as a believer?

2. Several years ago, gratitude journaling became popular as a way to help us remember and take note of our blessings. How is Israel's practice of linking memory to praise similar to the process of journaling our blessings? How might both spur us to praise?

3. What is your response to Psalm 137? Is your response different when you imagine these words spoken by a Holocaust survivor who has lost everything? How?

4. Psalm 137 refuses to minimize the evil of the dominating Babylonian war machine. What evils need to be named and taken seriously in our world, our communities, and our own lives? How can we pray honestly about those evils?

5. How often do you offer your anger toward others to God? Why do you think anger turns to hatred? How could praying that anger transform that process?

_____
_____
_____
_____
_____

6. As a follower of Jesus, what might you add to Psalm 137 that would both preserve the honesty of the prayer and reflect the ultimate truth that we are all broken sinners in need of redemption?

_____
_____
_____
_____
_____

7. How could Psalm 137, carefully placed in context, help encourage honesty in prayer—and ultimately healing—for a survivor of crime or abuse?

_____
_____
_____
_____
_____

8. When have you sensed God as the all-knowing, ever-present savior described in Psalm 139? How could you incorporate this powerful psalm into your regular prayer life?

_____
_____
_____
_____
_____

9. Do you ever wish—even for a second—for the destruction of people who do evil (139:19-24)? What is the difference between rejecting evil and rejecting those who do evil? How is praying for the transformation of evildoers and the end of evil different from and similar to these verses?

10. Why do you think the final psalms (146–150) are hymns of praise? How do they reflect our shared faith?

11. How does the book of Psalms as a whole honor both lament and praise? How can believers today honor both lament and praise in personal prayer and corporate worship?

12. What have you learned about the psalms through this study? What surprised you, challenged you, and encouraged you? How can you bring more authenticity to your personal prayer life?

Bibliography

Brueggemann, Walter. *The Message of the Psalms: A Theological Commentary.* Minneapolis: Augsburg Publishing House, 1984.

———. *Praying the Psalms: Engaging Scripture and the Life of the Spirit.* 2nd ed. Eugene OR: Cascade Books, 2007.

———. *The Psalms and the Life of Faith.* Ed. Patrick D. Miller. Minneapolis: Augsburg Fortress, 1995.

———. *Spirituality of the Psalms.* Minneapolis: Augsburg Fortress, 2002.

Brueggemann, Walter, and William H. Bellinger, Jr. *Psalms: New Cambridge Bible Commentary.* New York: Cambridge University Press, 2014.

Campolo, Tony, and Bart Campolo. *Things We Wish We Had Said: Reflections of a Father and His Grown Son.* Dallas: Word, 1989.

Davis, Ellen F. *Wondrous Depth: Preaching the Old Testament.* Louisville: Westminster John Knox Press, 2005.

Dawn, Marva J. *A Royal "Waste" of Time: The Splendor of Worshiping God and Being Church for the World.* Grand Rapids: Eerdmans, 1999.

deClaissé-Walford, Nancy L. *Introduction to the Psalms.* St. Louis: Chalice Press, 2004.

Edgerton, Clyde. *The Night Train: A Novel.* New York: Little, Brown and Company, 2011.

Goldhagen, Daniel Jonah. *Hitler's Willing Executioners: Ordinary Germans and the Holocaust.* New York: Alfred A. Knopf, 1996.

Greenstein, Edward L. "Introduction and Notes on Genesis." *HarperCollins Study Bible.* Ed. Wayne A. Meeks. New York: HarperCollins, 1989.

Keller, W. Phillip. *A Shepherd Looks at Psalm 23.* Grand Rapids: Zondervan, 1970, 2007.

Lerner, Harriet G. *The Dance of Anger: A Woman's Guide to Changing the Patterns of Intimate Relationships.* New York: Harper & Row, 1985.

Lester, Andrew D. *Coping with Your Anger: A Christian Guide.* Philadelphia: Westminster Press, 1983.

Mays, James L. *Psalms.* Interpretation: A Bible Commentary for Teaching and Preaching. Louisville: John Knox Press, 1994.

McBride, S. Dean, Jr. "Introduction and Notes on Exodus." *HarperCollins Study Bible.* Ed. Wayne A. Meeks. New York: HarperCollins, 1989.

McCann, J. Clinton, Jr. "Psalms." *New Interpreter's Bible*, vol. 4. Nashville: Abingdon Press, 1996.

Miller, Patrick D. "Introduction and Notes on the Psalms." *HarperCollins Study Bible.* Ed. Wayne A. Meeks. New York: HarperCollins, 1989.

Peterson, Eugene H. *Answering God: The Psalms as Tools for Prayer.* New York: HarperCollins, 1989.

———. *Eat This Book: A Conversation on the Art of Spiritual Reading.* Grand Rapids: Eerdmans, 2006.

———. *A Long Obedience in the Same Direction.* Downers Grove IL: InterVarsity Press, 1980.

———. *The Message.* Colorado Springs: NavPress, 2002.

———. *Working the Angles.* Grand Rapids: Eerdmans, 1987.

Rainwater, Robert. "Sheol." *Mercer Dictionary of the Bible.* Ed. Watson E. Mills. Macon GA: Mercer University Press, 1990.

Zenger, Erich. *A God of Vengeance? Understanding the Psalms of Divine Wrath*. Trans. Linda Maloney. Louisville: Westminster John Knox Press, 1996.

Study the Bible...
a book at a time

SESSIONS Series

Series Editor:
Michael D. McCullar

The *Sessions Series* is our expanding set of Bible studies designed to encourage a deeper encounter with Scripture. Each volume includes eight to ten lessons as well as resource pages to facilitate preparation, class discussion, or individual Bible study.

Sessions with Genesis
The Story Begins
by Tony W. Cartledge

Sessions with Samuel
Stories from the Edge
by Tony W. Cartledge

Sessions with Matthew
Building a Family of Faith
by William D. Shiell

Sessions with Mark
Following Jesus at Full Speed
by Michael D. McCullar
and Rickey Letson

Sessions with Luke
Following Jesus on the Journey
to Christian Character
by Timothy W. Brock

Sessions with John
The Vocabulary of Grace
by Robert B. Setzer, Jr.

SMYTH & HELWYS
Call **1-800-747-3016** to order.
Visit **www.helwys.com/sessions**

Also Available in the Sessions Series

Sessions with Corinthians
Lessons for the Imperfect
by Michael D. McCullar

Sessions with Galatians
Finding Freedom through Christ
by Eric S. Porterfield

Sessions with Philippians
Finding Joy in Community
by Bo Prosser

Sessions with Colossians & Philemon
On the Move with God
by Eric Porterfield

Sessions with Thessalonians
Being Faithful in a Confusing World
by Rickey Letson

Sessions with Timothy & Titus
Timeless Teachings for Leaders of Any Age
by Michael D. McCullar

Sessions with James
Explorations in Faith and Works
by Michael D. McCullar

Sessions with Peter
Discovering God's Encouragement for the Christian Journey
by Sarah Jackson Shelton

Sessions with John & Jude
God's Abiding Words for an Active Faith
by Charles Qualls